THE KEY TO THE TRUE KABBALAH

Volume III
Of The Holy Mysteries

FRANZ BARDON

THE KEY TO
THE TRUE KABBALAH

The Kabbalist as
A Perfected Sovereign in
The Microcosm and the Macrocosm

MMXVIII
Merkur Publishing, Inc.
Wisdom of the Occident

First Printing 2002, Second Printing 2007, Third Printing 2010, Fourth Printing 2011, Fifth Printing 2013, Sixth Printing 2015, Seventh Printing 2018

ISBN 9781885928146

Translated by Gerhard Hanswille
Title of the German original edition:
Der Schlüssel zur wahren Quabbalah

Edited by Kenneth Johnson

Printed in the United States of America

Merkur Publishing, Inc.
www.merkurpublishing.com

Dedication

My third book, which I worked on with a special preference, is dedicated with fatherly benevolence to my dear son Lumir, who, as a result of his prenatal education, has given me nothing but pure joy.

Note to the Reader

To achieve success in Kabbalah, it is advisable to learn the proper phonetic German pronunciation of the letters.

Contents

Part I
Theory

Part II
Practice

Part III
The Practice of Formula Magic

Preface

As promised in his two previous works, *Initiation into Hermetics* and *The Practice of Magical Evocation*, Franz Bardon has now published his third textbook, dealing with the cosmic language, called Kabbalah by the initiates.

Those who, through practical work, are already well advanced in their studies of spiritual, i.e. Hermetic, science, will be understandably filled with great joy and, on account of having already acquired practical experience, will be strengthened in their confidence that the path they have chosen is the most reliable one and will, without exception, meet all their expectations.

Many scientists whose interests have been stimulated in the Kabbalah begin their studies in accordance with the prevailing theories and instructions, though without having matured sufficiently through proper schooling. The contents of this, Bardon's third book, will astound them. If not at once, then certainly within a very short time they will have to admit that all the Kabbalistic methods specified herein differ essentially in their richness, variety and truthfulness from those contained in Kabbalistic books hitherto published.

Not even the most concealed, most secret libraries of secluded monasteries in the East, those ashrams which are inaccessible to ordinary mortals, can pride themselves on possessing the true Kabbalah in one single secret script of such clear and distinct wording. After a perusal of this book, even those who already have a good knowledge of the Kabbalah will concede that they have a good deal to catch up on before they can call themselves true Kabbalists. Upon careful consideration, the reader will be convinced that it is worth his while to forego all other incomplete teachings and work faithfully in his own interests with the methods in this textbook.

Throughout human history, many a Kabbalist has devoted his entire life to an exhaustive but fruitless search for the unpronounceable name of God lost by mankind in the days of yore. But having gone through this third work conscientiously, the Kabbalist will suddenly have the sense of a miracle accomplished, an immense treasure dropped into his lap by Divine Providence when, as a reward for his untiring, honest efforts, the long-lost true name of God (among many other things) will reveal itself to him. And this exceedingly high reward will be bestowed upon all those seekers of truth for whom these three volumes, unparalleled in spiritual literature, are not merely interesting reading but valuable study material which needs only to be implemented.

Otti Votavova
(April 11, 1903 – February 9, 1973)

Introduction

I have titled this work, the third in my series of books on initiation, *The Key to the True Kabbalah*. Strictly speaking, it is concerned with the theosophy of the knowledge of the Word. When engaged in theurgy, one must in any case have gone through magical development; one absolutely must have completely mastered every exercise described in my first volume *Initiation into Hermetics*. Like my first two works, the present book consists of two parts. In its first or theoretical part, I prepare the reader for the difficult task of working with the Kabbalah, whereas the second part contains the actual practice.

Much has been written about the Kabbalah (a difficult subject in Hermetic literature), but in practice only a little of it can be used. It has almost always been maintained that a person engaged in the practice of the Kabbalah must have a command of the Hebrew language, without which it is impossible to study the art. The theoretical Kabbalah, which comprises most of the extant writings, is primarily of Hebrew origin and is said to convey to the student an ideology of life in accordance with a Kabbalistic paragon. But the number of books about the practice and use of the true Kabbalah is very limited. A few rabbis knew the genuine Kabbalistic teachings, but, probably due to their orthodox thinking, kept it strictly confidential; thus not even fragments of Kabbalistic practice have become known to the public.

The many descriptions of Kabbalistic methods do not even offer any theoretical details to the serious student, to say nothing of any true points of reference for the practice. At most they supply a philosophical representation of the microcosm and macrocosm. The student of Kabbalah cannot obtain any idea whatsoever of Kabbalistic ideology, since on the one hand he is unable to find his way in this great confusion of opinions and on the other hand he is still in the dark due to the contradictory statements made in different books.

My present volume contains the theory as well as the practice, the latter being especially comprehensive, as the diligent student of Kabbalah will see for himself. To represent the whole Kabbalah comprehensively in a single book is, of course, impossible for technical reasons alone. However, I have made an effort to string together the pearls of this wonderful science so that they form an extremely beautiful chain. In so doing, I have naturally taken into account the laws of analogies in connection with the microcosm and the macrocosm, for if the whole spectrum of the Kabbalah is to be presented without any omissions, it cannot be done otherwise. I make as little use as possible of the numerous Hebrew terms which have, until now, been commonly employed in Kabbalah, and I have preferred such terms as may be easily understood by everybody. At any rate, the reader studying my book will gain quite a different idea (i.e. the right idea) of the practical Kabbalah.

Whoever desires success in convincing himself, through practical experience, of the reality of the Kabbalah must systematically work his or her way through my two first books, *Initiation into Hermetics* and *The Practice of Magical Evocation*. Otherwise, one's development upon the path to perfection will require too much time and any success will come too late. However, the reader may, if he chooses, study my books entirely from a theoretical point of view. In so doing, he will acquire a knowledge which no mere philosophical book can provide. But knowledge is not yet wisdom. Knowledge depends on the development of the intellectual part of the spirit; wisdom, on the other hand, necessitates the balanced development of all four aspects of the spirit. Therefore, knowledge is mere philosophy, which by itself alone can make a man neither a magician nor a Kabbalist. A learned man will be able to say a lot about magic, Kabbalah, etc., but he will never be able to understand the powers and abilities correctly.

With these few words I have explained to the reader the difference between the philosopher and the sage. It is up to the reader to follow the more convenient path of mere knowledge or to proceed along the more difficult path of wisdom.

Even primitive nations, regardless of race and habitation, had their particular religion or idea of God, and consequently some kind of theology as well. Every theology may be divided into two parts: an exoteric and an esoteric part, the exoteric teachings being intended for the common people and the esoteric knowledge being the theology of initiates and high priests. Exoteric teachings never contained anything of true magic or Kabbalah. Thus only magicians and Kabbalists could become the initiates of primitive nations.

Since time immemorial it has been a most sacred commandment to keep this wisdom strictly confidential; firstly in order to maintain authority, secondly in order not to lose power over the people, and thirdly in order to prevent any abuses. This tradition has been maintained up to the present day, and although my book will bestow complete knowledge upon the reader, it will give him only knowledge and not wisdom. He will have to attain the latter by honest practical work. The degree of wisdom he attains will depend upon his maturity and development. My book will reveal the highest wisdom only to the really mature, the chosen ones. There exists a great distinction between the learned man and the sage; therefore I am not trespassing against the commandment of silence, in spite of my publishing the highest truths and secrets. To the learned man, wisdom will always remain occult; to the chosen ones, it will be completely bestowed.

The science of the Kabbalah, or theurgy, is of extreme antiquity and has its origins in the Orient. Since time immemorial, the ancient sages have concealed their greatest secrets in a universal or metaphorical language, as may be seen from the hieroglyphics of the Egyptians and other ancient people. These sages knew how to pass on their teachings through metaphor, in a symbolic mode of expression. Hence the understanding of the teachings was always dependent upon the student's degree of maturity. The Oriental wisdom was documented only in symbolic language, and has consequently remained a secret to the immature or, in other words, to any person who has not reached the necessary degree of maturity by developing his individuality under the guidance of a master or guru. That is why, until today, all true initiatic writings agree that initiation is not only impossible but dangerous without a guru. A true initiate must make the teachings progressively understandable to the student from a symbolic point of view and instruct him in the language of symbolism, the original language, the metaphorical language. The student soon becomes accustomed to his master's language and, again, is able to pass on the wisdom only in this symbolic language.

Thus, up to the present day, this holy science has been passed on from one person to another by tradition alone. Any explanation a master gave to his student was conveyed to the latter through inspiration, so that the student understood his master through an experience of sudden realization. This enlightenment, i.e., initiation, has a number of names in the Orient, for instance *abhishekha, ankhur,* etc. Never did a master reveal the true mysteries of wisdom to the poorly prepared or the immature. There were, no doubt, also magicians and Kabbalists who left behind writings concerning the highest wisdom; but, as we have seen, such wisdom was laid down entirely in symbolic language, and if by chance it came into the hands of an immature person it remained incomprehensible to him. However, sometimes it happened that an immature person tried to explain this wisdom from his own point of view; that such an explanation was far from any true interpretation goes without saying. Most writers who have succeeded in getting hold of the writings of Oriental initiates have always made the same mistake: they have translated these writings into the language of the intellect, interpreting them literally. Since they did not possess sufficient spiritual maturity to interpret the symbols of a mystery or a practice correctly, and so on, due to a lack of necessary training and true understanding of the metaphorical or cosmic language, they have been responsible for numerous errors in Hermetics. Today hardly anyone can imagine how many absurd practices have been published in civilized languages.

In my present work I have translated the symbolic language into the language of the intellect, making accessible the path to the true Hermetic science of Kabbalah, the mystery of the Word, in a manner by which a knowledgeable person may safely proceed.

Franz Bardon

The Symbolism Of
The Third Tarot Card

The illustration on the opposite page is a graphic representation of the third Tarot card.

The first or outer circle has ten equal sections representing the ten Kabbalistic keys. These ten keys (note their color symbolism) are identical to the ten Hebrew Sephiroth.

Since these ten keys or Sephiroth encompass the knowledge of the whole universe with all its forms of existence, methods and systems, they occupy the outer circle.

The fact that these ten keys refer to the micro- as well as the macrocosm becomes evident also by the fact that the next or second circle depicts the signs of the universal zodiac, again in the corresponding color symbolism.

The third circle (going from the outside to the inside) is the planetary circle, as shown by the planetary symbols and including the colors analogous to the planets.

All three rings encircle a large square symbolizing the four elements, represented in the relevant color symbolism. This square, indicating the realization of the elements, symbolizes the material world.

The inner, smaller square signifies the mystery of Tetra-grammaton, the Jod-He-Vau-He or Kabbalistic four-letter key necessary in order to master the elements and their influences.

The sun in the center of the illustration represents Divine Providence, the Akasha principle, the origin of everything that exists.

Thus not only man (i.e. the microcosm) but the whole macro-cosm is graphically represented in this illustration. Furthermore, all keys are contained therein, the four-letter key being especially dominant since it is the key to the realization of things. Every-thing that the Kabbalah teaches us, i.e., its entire system and all its analogies, is clearly indicated in this illustration and the color symbolism. The meditating Kabbalist will therefore deduce all his analogies from the third Tarot card, and find that these few explanatory hints are completely sufficient.

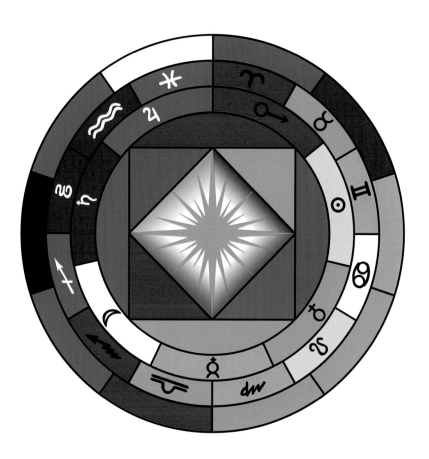

PART I

THEORY

The Kabbalah

The Kabbalah is the science of letters, of language and the Word — not, however, the language of the intellectual, but (mind you) the universal language. The term Kabbalah is of Hebrew origin; the various religious systems have different terms for this science. Thus, for instance, in India and Tibet the science of the Word is called Tantra. And again in other religious systems they speak of "formulas" and so on.

In my present work I will retain the term Kabbalah. To speak Kabbalistically is to form words from letters — words analogous to this or that idea according to the universal laws. Knowledge of the use of Kabbalistic language must be gained through practical experience. Kabbalah, therefore, is the universal language by which everything was created; it is the embodiment of one or several divine ideas. God created everything by means of the universal language of Kabbalah. John the Evangelist also refers to Kabbalah in the Bible when he says, "In the beginning was the Word: and the Word was with God." Thereby John clearly expresses the truth that God made use of the Word in order to create out of Himself.

Only he who is actually in a position to materialize the divinity within himself in accordance with the universal laws in such a way that he will speak, out of himself, as a deity, may be regarded as a true Kabbalist. The practicing Kabbalist, therefore, is a theurgist, a "god-man," capable of applying the universal laws in the same way as the macrocosmic God.

Just like the magician who, through the initiation he receives and the development he endures upon the path of perfection, has realized the connection with his inner deity and can now act accordingly, so does the Kabbalist as well, the only difference being that the Kabbalist makes use of the Divine Word externally as an expression of his divine spirit. Every true magician who has control of the universal laws can become a Kabbalist by acquiring knowledge of the practical Kabbalah. The structures of the Kabbalah cited in numerous books are quite suitable for the theorist who wants to get an idea of the lawfulness of the Kabbalah, but they are thoroughly insufficient as regards that practice which promises knowledge of the correct application of the powers of the Word.

Thus it is clear that a perfect Kabbalist must be a person connected with God, a person who has realized God within himself and who, being a god-man, makes use of the universal language whereby whatever he utters immediately becomes a reality. To whatever sphere he directs this language, there shall his utterance be realized. In India, for instance, a person who immediately realizes every spoken word is called a *vag*. In Kundalini Yoga this power and ability is identified with the Visuddha Chakra. A perfect Kabbalist knows everything concerning the lawfulness of the micro- and macrocosmic Word — by which the law of creation through the Word is to be understood — and he also knows what true harmony represents. Since, with his microcosmic language, he is representing the deity, a true Kabbalist will never violate the laws of harmony. If he acts contrary to the laws of harmony, he is no longer a true Kabbalist but a man of chaos. From the Hermetic point of view, a Kabbalist or theurgist is, in his own body, a representative of the macrocosmic deity on our earth. Whatever he, as God's representative, speaks in the original language will occur, for he has the same power as the creator, as God.

To achieve this maturity and pinnacle of Kabbalistic initiation the theurgist must first learn his letters like a child. In order to form words and sentences with them and, in time, to speak in the cosmic language, he must have a complete command of them. The methodology involved in this learning is dealt with in the practical part of this book.

Anyone, no matter which religious system he may adhere to, can occupy himself with the true Kabbalah, theoretically as well as practically. The Kabbalistic science is not a privilege of those who profess the Jewish faith. Hebrew scholars affirm that the Kabbalah is of Jewish origin, but in the Jewish mystical tradition itself the knowledge of the Kabbalah is said to be of ancient Egyptian origin. The history of the Hebrew Kabbalah, its beginnings and development, etc., may be found in the relevant literature on the subject, for much has already been written in this field.

In my book, I explain the synthesis of Kabbalah only so far as is absolutely necessary for the practice. I refrain from the unnecessary burden of history and other structural interpretations of Kabbalistic philosophy.

The term Kabbalah has often been abused by degrading it to a game of numbers, horoscopic assessments, name analogies and various other mantic devices. As the reader will learn from the practical part of this book, numbers do have a certain relationship to letters, although this is one of the lowest aspects of the Kabbalah, and one which we do not wish to deal with here. True Kabbalah is not a mantic science which makes fortune-telling possible, nor is it a form of astrology which facilitates the interpretation of horoscopes, nor is it an anagram, the construed names of which make prognosis possible.

Since true Kabbalah, when applied correctly, represents the universal laws, relevant analogies of harmony in accordance with cosmic analogies may, up to a certain point, be discerned. This, however, is ordinary fortune-telling and has nothing to do with the true science of the universal language.

The reader will agree that this science is most sacred, and will never dare to degrade the universal laws in order to fulfill ordinary mantic purposes. Each religious system had its own genuine Kabbalah which in time was lost due to the various reforms of the religious systems; it is being fully maintained by true initiates only in the Orient. The ancient Celts and initiated Druids also had their own genuine Kabbalah, well known to the Druid priests. The practical use of runic magic by the Druid temple priests can be traced back to ancient knowledge of the Kabbalah. Today there are unfortunately only a few people who understand the runic Kabbalah of the old Druids and can apply it practically. The practical runic Kabbalah has been lost completely during the course of time.

Man as Kabbalist

In my first book, *Initiation into Hermetics*, I divided man into three regions — body, soul and spirit. Also, I discussed the concept of the "tetrapolar magnet." Upon meditation, it will be clear to the student that the mental body is connected to the astral body by the mental matrix, and that the astral matrix keeps the mental and astral bodies together with the material body. It will also become clear that the physical body is kept alive by food (the condensed substance of the elements), while the astral body is sustained by breathing. The mental matrix links sense perception to the material and astral bodies. The aspiring Kabbalist must understand these concepts thoroughly and, if he seriously wishes to study the Kabbalah, must be able to gain a clear picture of these processes in his own body. Apart from this fundamental doctrine, the Kabbalist must acquire a deeper relationship with his own self, for these deeper relations form the actual basis for the study of the Kabbalah.

The activities and effects between body, soul and spirit come to pass automatically within every human being, whether or not he has been initiated into the secrets of Hermetic science. For the Kabbalist these activities and effects constitute the basics: he understands all the processes and is therefore able to arrange his life in accordance with the universal laws.

This knowledge distinguishes the initiate from the non-initiate; for the initiate, having been taught the exact meaning of the laws, knows how to make practical use of them and is able to equilibrate any disharmony in the body, soul and spirit. Apart from this, the initiate, through his conscious attitude towards the universal laws, is capable of leading a proper life in accordance with these laws, and of proceeding along the path to perfection. Seen from this perspective, initiation is something unique, offering a special ideology. For the initiate looks upon the world with eyes quite different than those of anyone else. Because he is an initiate, the various twists of fate to which he will eventually be exposed cannot harm him to the extent of causing him severe suffering. One may easily understand this, considering what has been said above.

From the Kabbalistic point of view, man is a perfect embodiment of the universe, for he has been created in the image of God. Man is the most superior being on our earth, and everything which occurs on a grand scale in the universe at large occurs on a small scale in man as well. Seen from the Hermetic point of view, man is the world in miniature, the microcosm, in contrast to the universe or macrocosm.

A true Kabbalist, one who genuinely wants to do practical work within the scope of the universal laws and who wants to take an active part in the Great Work, absolutely must have undergone magical development and must embody the true ideas in accordance with the universal laws. Whoever is content with mere theory will attain Kabbalistic knowledge and enrich the intellectual side of his spirit, but the other three fundamental principles of the spirit will lag behind. A theorist will never be able to grasp the essence of Kabbalistic knowledge properly, and much less will he be able to effectuate anything with it.

He may become a Kabbalistic philosopher if he possesses the intellectual abilities, but never a true, magically trained Kabbalist whose spoken word becomes reality. A theorist may become a scientist, but never a sage. The difference between a learned man and a sage is very great. The magician, because of his magical development, accomplishes his intentions through his will. But because the magician's relationship with God is on a different level than that of the Kabbalist, he cannot make use of the true magic word as can the Kabbalist. A magician who is not occupied with the practical Kabbalah may use those powers which he has developed within himself and may call various beings to help him with his work, but a Kabbalist can achieve everything through the Kabbalistic Word alone, without the aid of entities, genii, and so on.

Therefore, from the Hermetic point of view a true Kabbalist is the highest initiate, for he represents the divinity in the micro-cosm and, applying the laws of analogy, can become active in the macrocosm as well. This is the difference between the magician and the Kabbalist; therefore, anyone striving for perfection will want to occupy himself, in practice, with the Kabbalah. A Kabba-list taking part in the Great Work will typically be selected by Divine Providence to carry out certain missions. The true Kabba-list thus serves as a representative of creation, but he remains the most obedient servant of the universal laws; the more initiated he becomes, the more humble he is towards Divine Providence. Truly, he has been given the greatest power; yet he will never use that power for his own purposes, but only for the welfare of humankind. The true Kabbalist is the highest initiate, and from the universal point of view nothing is impossible for him, and any word he utters must, without exception, become a manifested reality.

I should like to point out once again the difference between a perfected human being, in other words a true initiate, as opposed to a saint. The true magician will not need this explanation, for he will understand everything from what has already been said here. Those readers, however, who read my books only theoretically may be told that a perfected human being acknowledges all universal laws, duly takes them into consideration in the macrocosm as well as in the material, astral and mental planes, and lives by them. The saint, on the other hand, is interested only in a particular religious system, and puts that system into practice in accordance with its dogmas and regulations, though not in every instance, i.e. not equally in every sphere.

He who strives towards saintliness alone usually neglects both the physical body and the material world, regarding them as *maya* or delusion, and consequently, after the relevant training, he releases only a few aspects of the universal laws which are within him. Such people do attain a climax in regard to those aspects of development which they have chosen as their goal — the divine love, compassion, or kindness which they realize within themselves. These people see the universal laws only from the point of view of their own spiritual development, but are unable to comprehend the complete picture of universal lawfulness, nor can they describe that lawfulness. From the point of view of Hermetics, such a path cannot be regarded as a perfect one and hence is merely termed "the path of saintliness." A true initiate or Kabbalist, on the other hand, will seek to acknowledge all divine aspects equally and to realize all of them successively. This way, of course, is longer and more difficult, and one incarnation is usually insufficient for completion. But the true initiate is not terribly anxious to attain his goal in one, or even several, incarnations, for time does not matter to him. The most important thing for him is the awareness that he is proceeding along the right path.

On the path to perfection there should be no haste. Everything needs its time and, above all, requires the maturity necessary for it to reach perfection. From the Hermetic point of view there are actually only two paths: the path to saintliness and the path to perfection. The path to saintliness has as many different systems as there are religions on earth. He who chooses the way to saintliness has decided to realize within himself only one or a few of the possible divine aspects, and hence is usually regarded by the world as symbolizing one relevant divine idea. With very few exceptions, saintliness even becomes a hindrance to both the saint and the world, for due to the time-consuming devotion of his disciples, worshippers, and followers, he is often impeded in his mission, task and ascent.

I do not want to deal here with those who consciously decorate themselves with a halo in order to be respected, adored, worshipped, etc. Unfortunately, there are a great number of such people in this world; a true saint retires to solitude, whereas a hypocrite will show off his halo. But he who takes the path to perfection will never seek solitude: he will remain in the place which Divine Providence has allocated to him and continue working at his personal development without drawing attention to himself. He will not do even the slightest thing which might display his magical maturity to the outside world. On the contrary, he may even try to disguise his attainments so as not to be bothered by the curious and the immature. This just goes to show that there is also a great difference in the attitude and behavior of a saint as opposed to a perfected human being: the saint will lose his own individuality as soon as he has reached his goal, but this is not the case with the perfected human being, for it is not his personal individuality which is at stake but his individuality as a god-man.

The Laws of Analogy

The laws of analogy have great significance in all true religious systems, including the science of Hermetics, and therefore play a most important role. In the universe, everything was created according to strict lawfulness, and that is why one thing leads to another with astonishing precision, like the most precise clockwork. In Hermetic science the study of the practical application of this lawfulness is called Kabbalah. All Hermetic systems and methods, all religious philosophies and systems which do not take, or only partly take, the universal laws into account, are one-sided and therefore imperfect. Religious systems that acknowledge only one aspect of the law and neglect all others, or even oppose them, can be of only limited duration, though their downfall may not come until after hundreds or thousands of years. Only those religious systems which take into account the absolute universal laws will exist permanently and remain for eternity.

All original divine ideas, e. g., absolute harmony, order, periodicity, etc., are reflected in the absolute lawfulness of the universal laws. The attentive reader will not have failed to notice that in my first book, *Initiation into Hermetics*, I have already illustrated a system for the development of the body, soul and spirit which is based on the universal laws and which represents the first initiation on the path to perfection. As one must conclude from the absolute laws, true initiation is neither a privilege of sects nor dependent upon any religious ideology. No special mention need be made of the fact that the comprehension of the fundamental truths, i.e., of the universal laws, necessitates a magical equilibrium in all three planes. Whoever strictly adheres to the universal laws in all three planes, who comprehends them clearly and masters them completely, is not only the master of his own small world but also a master in the universe. The practical initiation points the way, and especially the knowledge of the Kabbalah.

In the practical part of this book, I have published a system dealing with the practice of the Kabbalah in strict accordance with the universal laws. This system has existed for thousands of years and was already taught from mouth to ear in primeval times; later it was passed on in the schools of the prophets and in the temples of initiation of various nations and peoples. Knowing the laws of analogy, the initiate is able to achieve, in each plane, everything that is within the scope of lawfulness and harmony. The initiate may relate the law of analogy to any science, and he will always be right on target. If, for instance, a physician is a Hermetic, he is forthwith in a position to bring his medical knowledge into line with the universal laws as well, and, by the use of analogy, not only to find out disharmony (i.e., disease) and its cause, but also, and again by using the key of analogy, to prescribe the proper remedy for the removal of the seat of the disease. In respect to the great possibilities available to the informed, it may be worthwhile to do good not only unto oneself but especially to become active on behalf of suffering humanity. The same key of analogy can be used in any other field and will render equally good service to the individual as well as to humankind.

The expression "chaos," which people are so fond of using, is only a term of ignorance. In reality, God, the highest and unimaginable Creator, has formed everything precisely and lawfully in accordance with His lawfulness, and it is in this lawfulness and all its aspects that we may mostly quickly recognize God. God, as the universal principle or Supreme Being, is incomprehensible and unimaginable. Only through His division, from the creation of the universe, from His works, can one draw analogous conclusions which will allow us to obtain at least some idea of God's greatness and eminence.

The Hebrew rabbis attempted to convey knowledge of the Kabbalah, the lawfulness of the creation, in the *Book of Creation* or *Sepher Yetzirah.* Although the *Sepher Yetzirah* is of Hebrew origin, this does not mean that other people did not lay down the universal laws of the creation as well. Just as in the *Sepher Yetzirah,* we find the history of creation expressed in accordance with the universal laws in the *Bhagavad Gita.* There are yet other documents, as well as oral traditions, historic buildings and monuments, etc., which give either written or visual evidence of the universal laws of creation.

In ancient Egypt, for instance, Hermes Trismegistos understood the history of creation and the universal laws, which he preserved in the *Emerald Tablet of Hermes* with the motto: "That which is above is like that which is below." Hermes thus gives clear witness to the fact that the small world, man, was created in accordance with the great world, the universe. Innumerable examples could be given regarding the analogies of the universal laws, but these little hints shall suffice.

Most of the relevant analogies are contained in the practical part of this book, in which the Kabbalist is instructed in detail as to how, according to the universal laws, he may completely master the true language of the micro- and macrocosm and its practical application. In the human body, the analogies become clearly visible and may be precisely ascertained by numbers.

The fact that man has exactly ten fingers and ten toes, rather than six or three, also represents an analogy which I will explain in detail later on. The same is true of all the other analogies which the reader may find in (for example) the *Sepher Yetzirah*;

no practical analogy needed for the study of the Kabbalah will be omitted here. In the practical part of this book I shall also discuss thoroughly, from the point of view of esoterics, the individual letters with regard to the mental, astral and material worlds, which not only express sounds but also numbers and ideas.

The practitioner of Kabbalah will learn another method of mathematics and will be able to express ideas by way of numbers and, vice versa, to convert numbers into ideas; furthermore, he will lean to transform letters into numbers and to clothe letters in numbers. In so doing, he will learn to know his own self, and thus also God. The Kabbalist will understand the perfection of the laws. He will realize that good and evil, if understood literally, are merely religious expressions, while in reality both principles, the positive and the negative, are necessary, since one cannot exist without the other. The Kabbalist will always endeavor toward the positive but never hold the negative in disdain; rather, he will learn to master it, for the Creator has created nothing which is useless.

The Esoterics of Letters

The mystery of the Word, or, to speak more intelligibly, the mystery of the knowledge and true use of the Word, can be attained only through the highest existing form of initiation. At all times, he who has been called Master of the Word has been the highest initiate, the highest priest, the true representative of God. Every religious system, every initiation, regards the knowledge of the Word as the highest knowledge. Even with Jesus we find that His favorite disciple, John, was Master of the Word and thus of the Kabbalah, as is made clear in his gospel, wherein you may quite literally read: "In the beginning was the Word and the

Word was with God." No other disciple of Christ was so profoundly initiated into the mystery of the Word as was John. As Master of the Word, he was able to work the greatest miracles, and, as the Bible itself tells us, he was the only one among the disciples who died a natural death. He was able to accomplish this because he was a Kabbalist, a perfect Master of the Word; all the other disciples suffered a martyr's death. As history tells us, many other initiates had also been Masters of the Word thousands of years before John.

Every word consists of letters, and every letter expresses, from the esoteric point of view, an idea and thereby a power, attribute, etc., which, however, may be expressed not only by the letter alone, but also, through the universal law of analogy, by a number. Thus lawfulness is made understandable by numbers, and ideas come to light by letters. The meanings of each letter are analogous to the three worlds known to us. Since the Kabbalist is able to express the sense of an idea by means of letters, and since he is also aware of the relevant number which expresses the same idea, the letters have quite a different meaning for him than they have in intellectual language. Thus by universal law a letter is Kabbalistically evaluated. This knowledge of the universal laws renders it possible for the Kabbalist to express several trains of thought by means of letters, and thus by the numbers analogous to them. A word composed relative to the absolute laws and analogies of the corresponding letters and numbers is a Kabbalistic Word in the universal or cosmic language. To be able to form a Kabbalistic Word, one must have a precise and complete knowledge of the analogies of letters and numbers.

In the practical part of this book, the Kabbalist will learn the exact and proper use of a word composed according to the universal laws with regard to the mental, astral and material worlds and with regard to the elements. He will learn to express words, and subsequently sentences, not only intellectually but with his whole being. Only a word expressed in such a manner will have a creative effect. The correct pronunciation of the letters in one's spirit, in one's soul, and later on in one's body as well, is the actual foundation of practical Kabbalistic mysticism.

In order to become effective creatively, the Kabbalist must learn to speak like a child that can only babble at first, and later learn to pronounce single letters and words. The letters have their analogous significance which the Kabbalist must learn and master in the mental, astral and material worlds, and likewise in the various planes and hierarchies.

From this one can see that the theorist who is only able to think intellectually and who comprehends letters, words and sentences with his intellect alone, will never become a true Kabbalist. He will only be able to comprehend the Kabbalah from an intellectual or philosophical point of view and in accordance with his own state of maturity. The practicing Kabbalist, however, will be able to perceive and understand how to make practical use of the sense of every letter, of its idea and lawfulness (number), with his spirit, his soul, and, last but not least, his whole body.

The study of the Kabbalah begins with the esoterics of letters. When creating ideas out of His Own Self and dividing and arranging them into universal laws, God formed letters and, with the letters, numbers, which have an exact and analogous connection to one another and which represent the whole universe from the highest to the lowest. The assertion of Hermes Trismegistos, "That which is above is like that which is below," is substantiated from the Kabbalistic point of view. The letters which God used to create from within Himself, the ideas that pleased Him, are clearly explained in the *Book of Creation* or *Sepher Yetzirah*.

At the moment of creation, ten principle ideas came into being above all things, which, in the Kabbalah, are called the ten Sephiroth. The number 10 is a reflection of the number 1, which in turn is a reflection of God in His highest form and lowest emanation. Based on a knowledge of the law of analogy, the Kabbalist will understand what I meant when I pointed out that, in relation to the ten principle ideas, man has ten fingers and ten toes. At this point, the Kabbalist will surely have surmised a certain relationship or analogous connection between the divine principle ideas and the *Sepher Yetzirah*. The fact that each mathematical number on earth can be reduced to the figures 1 to 9 by addition (the sum of the digits) also has a Kabbalistically analogous coherence. In the Hebrew Kabbalah, the numerical combinations were a complete science, known as Gematria; however, I shall mention only the most basic essentials necessary for the practical application of Kabbalistic mysticism, as well as for the use of the Kabbalistic Word. Whoever is interested in the special numerical combinations regarding the verse lines in Hebrew literature may, if he so wishes, resort to the relevant literature.

The Cosmic Language

Some writers make mention of the cosmic language, which they sometimes term the Uranian language. It may well be that some letters of the cosmic language are known to and comprehended by them, but up to this day nobody has written about it in detail. The Hermeticist will know from what has already been said that the term "cosmic language" signifies the language of God or the language of Divine Providence. By this, God, as Universal Spirit, has created everything that exists in the universe, from the tiniest up to the greatest and highest, according to those unshakable laws by which God expresses His Own Self. Therefore we can only understand God by way of His lawfulness in the universe, and clothe the synthesis of His laws into words and give expression to Him as the Highest Original Principle comprehensible to mankind.

To understand the Kabbalah and to use it practically means comprehending the cosmic language on the basis of universal lawfulness. Thus the cosmic language is a language of the law, a language of might and power, and at the same time also a language of dynamics, of condensation, materialization and realization. Seen from the Kabbalistic point of view, to speak the cosmic language is to form and create within the scope of the universal laws. Only the initiate who understands and masters the universal laws in their absoluteness may avail himself of the cosmic language when dealing with human beings and beings of other spheres. To speak the cosmic language, to be truly creative, to represent God as His true image, is something that is only possible for someone who is able to concentrate in tetrapolar fashion. Why tetrapolar? I shall explain that in detail in the next chapter.

Consequently, the cosmic language is not the language by which spiritual beings make themselves understood to one another. The communication between spiritual beings, regardless of hierarchy, happens intellectually (mentally) by means of the socalled metaphorical language. The thoughts are transferred by symbolic images — acoustically, telepathically and emotionally — from being to being. The language of spiritual beings, being imperfect, is therefore only a partial aspect of the cosmic language; it is, magically speaking, not as effective as the true cosmic language, since spiritual beings do not make use of tetrapolarity when communicating. The cosmic language is the most perfect language that exists, for it is analogous to the laws; that is, it expresses the universal laws in their cause and effect. The cosmic language is therefore the great "Let it be."

The Magico-Kabbalistic Word
— Tetragrammaton —

In many writings of the Freemasons and other secret societies, the lost key or lost Word of God is much discussed. The rituals which were once practiced by these societies are now, for the most part, simply imitations, performed traditionally and without any understanding of their deeper sense in relation to the cosmic laws. Therefore the rituals which, at one time, were introduced and practiced by true initiates are naturally quite ineffective today, since the key to their correct application has been lost. The key to the rituals of all these societies was bound to get lost, since the rituals were lacking the mystery of the tetrapolar magnet. In fact, the magic word Jod-He-Vau-He is the tetrapolar magnet which has been lost and which has usually been paraphrased by the word "Tetragrammaton." The use of this key gave to the oldest mysteries of the Freemasons — and to all those other esoteric societies which were founded long ago by true initiates — their actual magic, power and might. However, the true initiates realized that the mysteries were, in many cases, being desecrated and that some people even abused them; therefore, they withdrew and confided the lost word only to the truly mature. Thus the true use of the word Jod-He-Vau-He has been gradually lost.

God, by way of His lawfulness, has given expression to the entire universe and to His Being in relation to creation with the tetrapolar magnet — in other words, with four letters. For these four letters the Hebrew Kabbalah chose Jod-He-Vau-He, symbolic of the Divine Name which it was not permitted to utter aloud and for which the terms "Tetragrammaton" or "Adonai" were often substituted.

Therefore the spirit of everyone who represents the perfect image of God in creation is tetrapolar as well and has, as previously stated, four fundamental principles analogous to the name of God. The first active principle, which is subject to the element of Fire, is the will (Jod); the second principle, subject to the element of Air, is the intellect (He); the third principle, subject to the element of Water, is feeling (Vau); and all three fundamental principles of the spirit, that is, all three elements together, form the fourth active principle, which finds its expression in consciousness and is analogous to the element of Earth. In Kabbalistic terminology this fourth principle is expressed by the second He.

The Kabbalist will now have gained perfect clarity regarding the lawful sequence of reasoning and will realize that, in Hermetic science, all systems of development which do not teach the four basic principles of the spirit cannot be regarded as universal and are therefore imperfect, regardless of their methodology. It will be clear to the Kabbalist why, in my first book, *Initiation into Hermetics,* I discussed the Kabbalistic Jod-He-Vau-He in relation to the development of body, soul and spirit; at the same time, the reader will be convinced that the system of development recommended by me and containing the absolute lawfulness is perfectly correct.

The symbolic or talismanic interpretation of the word Jod-He-Vau-He is merely a graphic representation of the emanation of God in His highest form and represents the use of the universal laws. In the practical part of this book I shall describe the application of the four-lettered name of God. The tetrapolar magnet, the Jod-He-Vau-He, is the basic key, the highest Word of creation representing 4, the number of realization. From the number 4 emanates the lawfulness in every science, and every science is therefore analogous to this number.

The Kabbalistic Jod-He-Vau-He, the tetrapolar magnet in the universe, is usually symbolized by an equilateral quadrangle, a genuine square. Seen from the Hermetic point of view, the square is thus a symbolic record of the manifestation or creation by God. The number 4 has many analogies — the plus and the minus, the four created elements, the Kabbalistic number 4 which is attributed to the planet Jupiter and which symbolizes wisdom, the four points of the compass. Whatever analogies the Kabbalist may draw, he will always come to the surprising conclusion that the number 4 can be brought into relation to everything in the world as far as materialization is concerned.

I shall refrain from quoting any further correspondences of the number 4 and simply point out once again that the Kabbalist who adheres to my teachings and explanations may apply the key word of the number 4 in all cases where the realization or expression of lawfulness is concerned. There is no doubt that in the Kabbalah the number 4 also symbolizes the material plane. Not only does the Hermetic science of the West use the number 4 as a basis; the same principle also finds expression in the wisdom of the East. For instance, in Kundalini Yoga the Muladhara Chakra, the coarsest center of human awakening, is represented by a square, in one corner of which an elephant symbolizes the greatest and strongest land animal in the world. Through this it is covertly pointed out that the number 4 is the idea which serves as the starting point for a yogi's spiritual development. I have devoted a special chapter to the Muladhara Chakra in my book *Initiation into Hermetics*. I mention it again here only to make the Kabbalist remember that the original wisdom of the entire earth, whether you search for it in the Orient or in the Occident, was always, when understood rightly, in full harmony with the Jod-He-Vau-He.

Thus Divine Providence has used the tetrapolar magnet, the fourfold principle, in the highest Word of the creation, and by so doing has expressed universal lawfulness with regard to His Own Self. Both numerically and from the tetrapolar standpoint, Jod-He-Vau-He is the highest Word that can be pronounced; from it

God also created other basic principles whereby multi-numerical magico-Kabbalistic words came into existence, which again exemplify further basic ideas and consist of further numbers, but which always have an inherent relationship to the number 4. Of course, there are also Kabbalistic words with the numbers 5, 6, 7, 8 and 9 which as basic ideas represent divine emanation. Apart from the name of God composed of the four letters Jod-He-Vau-He, there are other Kabbalistic key words consisting of five, six, seven and eight letters, each representing a basic principle. In the Hebrew Kabbalah there are also (apart from the name of God expressed by the four letters Jod-He-Vau-He, the so-called Tetragrammaton) names for God consisting of five, six, seven, and even one composed of twelve letters, which, however, may be reduced to a single basic idea by adding the sum of the digits. The so-called Shemhamephorash of the Hebrew Kabbalah, which expresses the name of God in seventy-two letters and may be used in various directions, may be reduced to the number 9 by adding the digits comprising 72, i.e. 7 + 2 = 9. Also, the cardinal number 9 has a correspondent relationship to the Jod-He-Vau-He, to number 4. This Kabbalistic analogy will immediately be clear to the Kabbalist.

The Shemhamephorash, however, is not solely of Hebrew origin; it is also mentioned in Egyptian and Indian records. This is verified in the Book of Thoth, the ancient record of Egyptian wisdom which is veiled in the Tarot. Hermes Trismegistos, too, as one of the oldest sages and most deeply initiated individuals of ancient Egypt, clearly shows this in his *Emerald Tablet* and in the *Book of Laws*. Likewise, when the Christian hierarchy was first established, it respected the Kabbalistic laws and brought the Christian religion, with all its particular symbols, into accord with the universal laws in a correspondent manner. Thus the number 4, the Jod-He-Vau-He, is symbolized by the four evangelists; furthermore, the twelve disciples are depicted by the signs of the zodiac, by which the number 3 is expressed at the same time, for 3 x 4 = 12. Furthermore, the seventy-two disciples of Christ are related to the Shemhamephorash and have a secret connection to the number 9, the highest number of the primeval divine emanation (7 + 2 = 9). It would be outside the scope of this book if I were to cite all the religions which have existed or still exist in our world, bringing them into a correspondent relationship with the ten principle ideas. It is up to the Kabbalist to make his own investigations, should he be interested in such details. I have just given him a hint of some importance which he should not disregard.

The Mantras

Many readers will certainly be interested in the question as to whether Mantra Mysticism constitutes a kind of Oriental Kabbalistic science. Even those who have already investigated yoga and have studied some yogic systems often have no clear picture of the mantras and Tantras or of Oriental Kabbalistic science. It would be well beyond the scope of the present volume to publish a complete treatise on the mantras; therefore I shall confine myself to explaining mantras from the Hermetic point of view.

None of the many varieties of mantras have anything to do with the cosmic language to which the Kabbalist is introduced in this book. Mantras are phrases which contain an idea or even a number of ideas in a single sentence, the so-called mantric formula, and which display the power or attributes of a particularly revered deity. We may therefore regard all mantras as prayers and make practical use of them as aids to meditation. Mantras are not magic formulas and do not bring forth magical or any similar powers. Mantras are expressions of ideas which serve the devotion to or connection with the relevant power, existence, might, attributes, and so forth. In the Orient, anyone using mantra is called a mantra yogi, regardless of which path of knowledge he has chosen and whether he is engaged in Hatha Yoga, Raja Yoga or some other yogic system.

Mantra Yoga is the application of devotional formulas for deities and their aspects. Not only does Indian philosophy teach mantras, but every other religion as well. In Christianity, for example, mantras are represented by the litanies. Mantras exist not merely to honor a deity, but to establish an intimate connection with that deity or to express a divine idea with a few words. The deity or being to be worshipped is up to the individual and will depend on his mental, psychic and karmic development. It is all the same whether the initiate worships Brahma, Vishnu, Buddha, Adi Buddha, Christ, Allah, and so on, for names are of no consequence at all. It is, however, important that the worshipper acknowledge and revere the basic principles of the deities in the form of their universal attributes, irrespective of the different aspects. Mantras are thus adjusted to the religious attitude of the individual. From the Hermetic point of view, it is not recommended to use the mantras of religions that are unknown to the Hermeticist. If someone were to use the mantras of a deity that is foreign or unappealing to him, such an application would be without purpose. Usually it is the unattainable, the inconceivable, the unapproachable, the unknown that will attract a European, and thus he will throw himself into something like Mantra Yoga and, by repeating a mantra, worship a deity to whom he is not actually drawn at all. He is usually induced to this practice by assertions, contained in quite a number of books on mantra, that the relevant deity will shower a worshipper with gifts provided he uses the appropriate mantra.

If a religious Christian should for some reason decide that

mantras of the Indian kind may be of use to him, but if, at the same time, he lacks the proper religious attitude towards the divine characteristic expressed by the relevant mantra, he will develop an inner conflict and be unable to penetrate into the power sphere of the associated deity, and thus will have little or no success. If, however, a Christian mystic has sufficiently strong religious belief, he will be able to form a mantra of his own which will contain the power, nature, and attributes of the deity he is adoring, regardless of whether he repeats this mantra in an Oriental language or in his mother tongue; in mantric mysticism it is most important that the symbolic idea of God should be expressed in a single phrase. If a Hermetic should find an Oriental deity appealing to him, and if he is unable to devote himself sufficiently to a religious system and deity of Western origin, he may feel free to devote himself to such an Eastern deity. This may also be an indication that the individual must, in one of his former incarnations, have already lived within the religious sphere which he has now chosen. Since the true magician is clairvoyant, he can, if he wishes and if it is of interest to him, take a retrospective glance with his spiritual eye into his former incarnations and ascertain whether this is true.

There are two basic types of mantras, the dualistic and monistic, the use of which is dependent, in each case, on the type of spiritual development and the goal towards which one is striving. The basis of a dualistic mantra is that the deity being worshipped is revered externally rather than internally, whereas mantras of the monistic type make it possible for the worshipper to unite with the deity or idea he adores, not externally but within himself, so that the devotee himself has a sense of being a part of or even identical to the deity.

Dualistic mantras, however, may have monistic characteristics such as personifying the adored deity, either within the individual or outside of him. Such mantras are called *saguna mantras* in

India. On the other hand, mantras expressing abstract ideas, universal attributes with which the worshipper identifies himself, are called *nirguna mantras*. In India the neophyte works with *saguna mantras* until he is sufficiently developed to form abstract ideas and use them in a mantric or nirgunic sense.

Hindu and other Oriental writings point out that one should not deal with Mantra Yoga unless one has chosen a suitable teacher or guru for this purpose. Only the true guru who is proficient in mantric mysticism is capable of teaching his pupil a mantra which corresponds to his state of maturity. In a situation like this, the teacher will also give his pupil the proper explanation of a mantra and its symbolic meaning. He initiates the neophyte, so to speak, into the power of the Word, into the mantras, and explains to him the practical analogous relations of the mantra to its corresponding deity. While the pupil is being given the explanations of the mantra by his guru, he will suddenly comprehend its secret meaning fully, and learn to understand the deity he worships. In the Indian terminology, this enlightenment or initiation into the corresponding mantra is called *abhishekha* in mantra yoga. On receiving the *abhishekha* from his guru and learning to understand the correspondences, the student immediately becomes capable of contacting the deity designated to him by mantric mysticism, whether it be the sagunic (dualistic) or nirgunic (monistic) type of mysticism. This is not to say that the mature pupil cannot work with the appropriate mantra of adoration unless he has the help of a teacher familiar with mantric mysticism, but it will take some time before he can comprehend the universal relationships and have success in his exercises.

In the texts of Mantra Yoga, mention is also made of the *guru mantras*. The term *guru mantra* has a double meaning: first, it refers to a mantra which is explained to the mature pupil by a guru through *abhishekha* (here we may be dealing with various different types of mantra, all of which relate to the attainment of one goal); second, the expression may indicate a type of mantra which the guru himself once used for a certain purpose and which he has made especially effective through years of repetition. It cannot be doubted that a mantra like this, when confided to the pupil, is as powerful and mighty for him as for the guru. Such a mantra will, of course, only be transferred from guru to pupil by way of oral tradition and never confided to anybody else.

To describe in detail each mantra, whether sagunic or nirgunic, whether Hindu, Buddhist or otherwise, as well as its application and purpose, is not the goal of this book; anyone who is interested will find ample instructions in the translated Oriental literature on Mantra Yoga.

Many mantras have to be repeated — whether whispered, spoken aloud, or only in the mind — after having taken up special positions or asanas, and have no other purpose than to retain in one's spirit, through repetition, the idea expressed by the mantra and not to be diverted from it. Many books also recommend that the mantra be spoken aloud in case of any disturbing influences, thus enabling one to concentrate more intently on the mantric idea. Of course, those mantras which are whispered repeatedly have a greater effect than those which are uttered aloud; however, the greatest effect is achieved by the mantras which are repeated only in one's mind.

To get an overview of the number of repetitions in mantric exercises, a rosary, string of pearls or beads (*tesbik* string) may be used as an aid, and at each repetition a pearl or bead of the rosary is pushed forward between two fingers and the thumb. The complete circuit of a Tibetan rosary with 108 pearls is called a *lhok*. It is of mystical and Kabbalistic significance that a *lhok* should have 108 pearls and not just 100. 108 adds up to 9 (1 + 8 = 9); 9 is the number of rhythm, and rhythm is uninterrupted motion. In Oriental terminology, 108 has yet another significance. It is, at any rate, analogous to Hermetic science. Anyone who is interested may refer to the Oriental literature. It is a well-known fact that mantras may be brought into relationship with diverse rituals and ideas, whether of the sagunic or nirgunic type, and therefore I need not go into detail here. Every religious system makes use of the same methods for its rituals, prayers and mantras which either serve the purpose of worshipping the divine ideas, attributes, etc., or of uniting with them, or of applying them practically for other purposes.

In some books, the *biju mantras* or *bindu mantras* are discussed as well. These mantras do not express any divine idea in the intellectual language, but are letters composed in accordance with the universal laws and formed into a word which cosmologically expresses an idea in accordance with the laws. Hence a *biju mantra* is of Tantric origin and, from the Hermetic point of view, may be regarded as Kabbalistic. The correct pronunciation of *biju mantras* — for example, the well-known mantras of the elements, the so-called tattwas: Ham, Ram, Pam, Vam, Lam, Aum, etc., — is confided to the pupil by his guru by means of an *abhishekha.* If the teacher imparts the *abhishekha,* he will at the same time show his pupil how to energize a mantra and how to use it in tetrapolar fashion later on.

The same is true in Tibetan Buddhism, where the Tantras of the five elements are symbolized by the *biju* formulas kha, ha, ra, va, a, and explained to the mature pupil for practical use. When applying the mantras, one may resort to many other aids in order to make things more easily understood, for instance prayers, purifications, and offerings, all of which serve the purpose of elevating the pupil's mind to the plane which corresponds with that of the deity.

From what has been said, it should be clear that the initiate understands what the mantras really are, whereas the layman may see in them something entirely different.

Finally, I should like to direct the reader's attention to those Oriental monks who use so-called prayer wheels for their meditations. These prayer wheels are devices similar to phonograph records on which mantras, and possibly Tantras, have been recorded and which are repeated a thousand times, or occasionally over a hundred thousand times, simply by turning the wheel. These monks believe that their progress on the way to supreme blissfulness will be the greater the more often they reel off the mantra or Tantra by turning the wheel. If such a prayer wheel is regarded only as an aid to the Buddhist monk in his concentration exercises, and if the wheel is used like the rosaries or strings of beads of the Hindu mantra yogis, then this concept may have some foundation from the Hermetic point of view. But when a monk recites his mantra thoughtlessly, when his mind is engaged in something else, he fails in his objective, and the true initiate will see in such a person a mere religious fanatic or sectarian and will sincerely pity him.

The Tantras

What Kabbalah is to the Occidental, Tantric science is to the Oriental, especially in India, Tibet, etc. The Westerner can only understand this science fully if he completely adopts the Oriental way of thinking and behavior, and this is seldom the case. The initiates of the Orient keep their secrets carefully hidden and are very taciturn when confronted by Westerners. If it is possible now and then to meet an initiate, he will usually say nothing about his secrets, or will express himself symbolically, or perhaps give small hints once in a while. But it is rare for an Occidental to receive an *ankhur* or even an *abhishekha* by an initiate of the Orient. Historically, yoga has been more accessible to Westerners than the

Tantras. The practical use of the Tantras is especially strictly guarded by the initiates, for Tantra Yoga is the most secret science, the manuscripts of which are concealed from the public like shrines in different monasteries, the so-called ashrams. Thousands of Tantric writings have accumulated in various monasteries over the course of time. However, some students, after passing difficult examinations in order to determine their maturity, are given access to these manuscripts.

Since my purpose in this book is to describe the practical Kabbalah, and since, for technical reasons, it is impossible also to deal with the Tantric science in detail, I will merely mention some principle aspects of the latter. However, the experienced Kabbalist will, if he so chooses, be able to succeed in the practice of Oriental Tantra on account of his knowledge of the laws of analogy and the Tetragrammaton key. The Oriental way of thinking regarding religion and ideology is a basic condition for the study of the Tantras. Should this be foreign to the Kabbalist, he will pay no special attention to Tantrism. In any event, what the Tantric will achieve by means of the Tantras, the experienced Kabbalist will achieve by means of the Kabbalah. There are no differences in this.

It should, however, be noted that the Oriental schools, and especially the Tantric Buddhists, for instance in Tibet, use the Tetragrammaton or fourfold key when applying the Tantras; thus the tetrapolar magnet I have described is used in the East as well as the West. The five revered Dhyani Buddhas are nothing other than correspondences of the five elements and their principles. The Tantric Buddhist, working with his mandala, knows that each deity, each Dhyani Buddha, represents not merely an element but an abstract divine idea, or even a number of such ideas, which correspond to that element. In Tantra there exist particular formulas for each element which are understood by the Tantric who is working with them. In the Buddhist school, the so-called

Vairocana Mantra, A - Va - Ra - Ha - Kha, is tetrapolar, i.e., Tetragrammatonic:

> A is attributed to Earth
> Va to Water
> Ra to Fire
> Ha to Air, and
> Kha to Ether.

In the Hindu Tantras the elements have the following formulas:

> Lam = Earth
> Vam = Water
> Pam = Air
> Ram = Fire
> Ham = Akasha

The student of Tantra will be taught by an experienced Tantric guru regarding the practical employment of a universal Tantra tetrapolarly in all planes and spheres. Only such a guru is able to bestow upon the student the true *abhishekha*, i.e., to truly initiate him. But in order not to shorten our description of Kabbalistic doctrines, I must refrain from a detailed explanation of the *abhishekha* in Tantra Yoga.

The Kabbalist will realize from all these statements that the Tetragrammaton key plays a very important role in all things, even in the most secret mysteries, and furthermore that it is applied by all systems and may therefore be regarded as the absolute key to true realization.

In Hindu teachings the elements are symbolized by deities. Also, the goddesses Maha-Swari, Maha-Kali, Maha-Lakshmi and Maha-Saraswati are universal abstract symbols of ideas which, in certain respects, relate to the elements. Detailed information concerning the symbolic attributes of the different deities with regard to the Tetragrammaton key will be found by the interested Kabbalist in any book on Oriental iconography. The Tantras are comprised of the same material as the Kabbalah, i.e., the practical use of letters, their laws and analogies with regard to the different planes. As with the Kabbalah, Tantra Yoga has both simple and compound Tantras which, considering cause and effect, may be used in all planes and applied in practice. Thus there also exist Tantric formulas which may be used for evoking mental, astral and material powers, for causes or other magic tasks. To go into detail would certainly exceed the scope of this book. Each true name of a higher being or deity has, when considering its attributes, ideas and effects, its Tantric or Kabbalistic analogy, and is typically represented symbolically by the picture of the deity.

Therefore, you will find that some goddesses have several hands, with the symbolic representation of an attribute in each hand. Thus, for instance, the goddess Maha-Lakshmi has four hands and in each hand she holds the symbol of an idea that corresponds to part of her nature. In one of her right hands she holds a lotus flower, the symbol of purity, beauty, love and divine knowledge. The front right hand displays a gesture of blessing as a symbol of protection, will and might. In one of her left hands she holds a sheaf, expressing the idea of abundance. In her fourth hand she holds a money purse, symbolically expressing the idea of wealth and prosperity.

The Tantric name of each deity is revealed to a Tantric apprentice only by a true guru. This is done by means of the *abhi-shekha* and under the seal of secrecy. With the help of the Tantras, the student may connect with the deity he has chosen and work practically with the powers assigned to her.

If they are to have true magical power, Tantric exercises must be practiced for years before the student becomes qualified to apply the Tantra practically and release the desired magical effect.

In the entire Orient there are only few yogis who are completely initiated into Tantric science. On the other hand, much mischief and mysticism has been attributed to the Tantras. Only one who has been initiated into Tantra Yoga can fully explain a Tantra to a student by making him acquainted with all the analogies of the respective ideas and by gradually teaching him how to pronounce the Tantra correctly with full spiritual consciousness. The guru teaches his student to do the same things a Kabbalist must be able to do, namely to apply the Tantra in tetrapolar fashion.

Every Tantric, whether Oriental or Occidental, must be capable without exception of pronouncing the Tantra with the four fundamental attributes of his spirit — will, intellect, feeling and consciousness — and becoming aware of the respective idea. The method of such pronunciation in Kabbalistic form for those who do not adhere to any Oriental religion or ideology will be taught in detail in this book.

In the Orient, the gullibility of the people (who are strongly predisposed to religion anyway) is often misused. There are many so-called masters who pretend to be Tantrics or yogis but who in reality have not the faintest idea of the true laws and analogies and who desecrate this high science for personal gain. Many Europeans, deluded by such mysticism, have, as a consequence, made great mistakes by taking literally that which is meant to be taken only symbolically. If Oriental instructions which are only to be understood symbolically are later translated into an intellectual language without commentary and without an *abhishekha*, great errors are caused, apart from all the mischief that has been played with Hermetic science over the course of time. The genuine Oriental books, therefore, rightly warn each student not to take the road of spiritual development without a guru, for only a true guru is in a position to explain to the student the secret meaning of the yogic systems and Tantric methods.

Sorcerers' Formulas

In this work I will also comment on magic formulas, firstly because they have a certain relation to the Kabbalah and secondly because I want the true Kabbalist to understand what a magic formula really is and how it differs from Tantric, mantric and other formulas. There are Tantric sorcerers' spells which are based on the universal laws but which are used primarily for selfish purposes on the material plane. These spells are designed in strict accordance with the universal laws and each letter contains a formula corresponding to lawfulness regarding cause and effect. Also, the sorcerer must use the formula which has been confided to him in a tetrapolar fashion if he wants to bring about the desired effect.

Furthermore, there are formulas which have been confided to the sorcerer by certain entities but which have nothing to do with true Tantric formulas. Since the sorcerer has received them from a being, such formulas do not necessarily have to conform to the universal laws. When such a formula is used, it is usually not the formula itself which brings about the desired effects but the respective being and the servants subject to it. I have written in detail about this in my second book, *The Practice of Magical Evocation.*

Another type of sorcerers' formula is the one used ritually by several people for a certain purpose, thus creating a battery or volt which releases the desired effect in the invisible world. This type of sorcerers' formula can be used by people with no spiritual training, but its disadvantage lies in the fact that he who uses it will be spiritually tied to the respective power sphere so strongly that he will hardly be able to free himself from it again. The use of such spells is therefore dangerous and is not recommended to the Kabbalist.

There exists still another type of sorcerers' formula: the type by which a single word — whether it expresses an aspect of universal lawfulness or whether it simply appeals to the respective idea — is so often repeated that it becomes dynamically effective and releases the desired effect. No special mention need be made of the fact that such dynamization will require much time and patience.

Thus there are Tantric, i.e. universal, sorcerers' formulas of a lawful character, and relative sorcerers' formulas created by an individual or by several people. As mentioned previously, a sorcerer's formula usually serves a personal purpose, whether it be the accumulation of wealth and power, the control over other beings, or whatever. It goes without saying that sorcerers' formulas may also be used in other planes to carry out tasks for egotistical motives, and it does not matter if the effects bring forth a being, a volt, or any other power.

There are no sorcerers' formulas for high spiritual purposes as such. In such cases, there are only Kabbalistic or Tantric compilations which may also be regarded as a kind of formula. These compilations contain a very specific universal lawfulness, and one must, of course, make use of the Tetragrammaton key whenever they are employed.

The numerous formulas in medieval grimoires which deal with the invocation of demons and other negative beings have nothing to do with the pure and true Kabbalah or the pure and true Tantra. These sorcerers' formulas either originate with entities or were formed on the basis of ritualistic, voltic powers. Any true magician or Kabbalist will consider it beneath his dignity to occupy himself with sorcerers' formulas of any kind. I have felt it my duty to write about this for the reader's information and to prevent any confusion by explaining the difference between a Tantra and a sorcerers' formula. The sorcerers' formulas which appear in fairy-tales in connection with wizards, witches and so on naturally embody a bit of true Hermetics, for fairy-tales are not just tales; they are symbolic representations of many Hermetic mysteries. For someone who has been initiated into magic and Kabbalah, who understands the symbolic language and who consequently looks upon everything with different eyes than those of an untrained person, fairy-tales will reveal many mysteries. A Hermetic will not be surprised by his childhood fondness for fairy-tales, and will still like to reflect on their contents in later years, for he understands their high and true sense which can only be found by reading between the lines.

Theory of Kabbalistic Mysticism

I have already pointed out several times that the interpretation of Oriental books on yoga, Tantra and other spiritual subjects is insufficient, and I have emphasized that nearly all writers who have translated these works into Western languages have not considered the fact that their contents are to be understood symbolically. A true Hermetic will find it easy to differentiate between symbolic and intellectual language. He will never translate Oriental writings literally and will always comprehend the true sense of the teachings, especially of the Hermetic science, and will work it out for practical use. Therefore, the many books written on Kabbalah, mysticism, and so on have been either partly or completely misunderstood, and have been passed on in the same way. Since numerous works have been written on Hermetic science throughout the centuries, most of them of Oriental origin, and since one translator has received the science from another, sometimes changing it speculatively, it is easy to see how the true laws and the true science have become more and more unintelligible. Thus this science has become genuinely "occult," or has been lost almost completely in the course of time.

Through the ages, many mystic societies have been founded which, naturally, all claim to have been initiated into the true science. A genuine magician, however, will never tie himself to any society — whatever name it might have — by oaths and the like; he will remain free from any such worldly fetters in order to proceed on his spiritual path without any appreciable constraints on his authority. In all true circles of initiation, the master is the teacher and friend of the pupil and will never use his authority to influence his student's spiritual path or coerce him into acknowledging the master's own authority. Wherever any kind of constraint is exercised upon the seeker, whether by means of oaths or other obligations, one can almost always assume that the true science is not being taught. Much could be said about this subject, but this reference will be enough to make the reader realize that the numerous mystic societies around the world are not always the place where one may gain the purest and most perfect knowledge, and that a student must always strive to travel his own path on the road to initiation. The basic motives behind many such societies are usually financial, and their members will sooner or later gain the sad experience that therein they will attain anything but true knowledge.

Above all, the Kabbalist is interested in the practical application of the universal Word, and thereby the use of letters, which leads to comprehension of the cosmic language. The origin of Kabbalistic mysticism is to be found in the East and dates back to ancient times. Right from the beginning of mankind, initiates have passed on the Kabbalistic mysticism by tradition from one culture to another.

Recently, the mysticism of letters as propounded by J. B.

Kerning[1] has found many interested followers. Kerning's concept of this mysticism also originates in the Orient. From a religious point of view, he relies upon the Bible, as when he interprets symbolically, through letter mysticism, Christ's washing of His disciples' feet. It is not my intention to criticize Kerning's system. Everybody should act according to his personal conviction and remain with the system he has chosen, if nothing better is accessible to him. A true Hermetic will not draw any connection between letter mysticism and Christ's washing of His disciples' feet, for this has quite a different meaning from the Hermetic point of view; it indicates that each individual has to begin his personal development from the lowest sphere or plane of the earth.

Unfortunately, very little has been written in the civilized world regarding the mysticism of letters; therefore, no one has a clear idea of its correct usage. The teachings of Kerning which involve spelling letters in one's feet cannot be recommended from the Hermetic point of view. The Hermetic will see at once the reason for this; for when the letters are concentrated in one's feet, one's consciousness must be transferred there as well, and any transfer of consciousness, whether into the feet or any other part of the body, leads to an unnatural vascular congestion. Whether the means to this end be letters or simple or compound words, names of deities or whatever, is of no consequence. By transferring one's consciousness into the feet, and by concentrating on them, a heat is produced which mystics may erroneously regard as the mystic fire itself. This transfer of one's consciousness has psychological and physiological side effects and the like which are also erroneously taken for mystical experiences, i.e. for certain states of the soul and spirit.

---

[1]A German mystic.

When practicing Kerning's exercises, a person of good and strong character who possesses moral virtues and pursues high ideals may not lose his equilibrium or perceive within himself at that moment any psychological disharmonies and so forth. But one who lacks strong character and good health, and thus has little power of resistance, may suffer serious harm to body, soul and spirit through such a one-sided system.

Should a student wish to apply Kerning's mysticism of letters practically from a Hermetic standpoint, he must first be in perfect physical, astral and spiritual equilibrium, and his will, intellect and feelings must have been trained and strengthened by continuous concentration exercises so that he has entirely mastered the three elements of Fire, Air and Water, in order to be able to operate with his consciousness without any danger. Whoever has equilibrated these three elements in his body, soul and spirit, and has attained a certain degree of stability, will not be content with an inadequate system such as this. Equipped with these abilities, he is already on the way to perfection; his intuition will show him the path to lawfulness.

The danger of creating an imbalance through one-sided mystical exercises involving letters is so much the greater with fanatics. I have met many people whose brief or prolonged exercises in the mysticism of letters sooner or later resulted in mental disturbances due to a one-sided transfer of consciousness. I was able to restore to these people their equilibrium through magical influence and save them from suffering any further damage to their health. Letter exercises focused in one's feet lead to a split personality — schizophrenia and all its serious consequences. A true seeker will not deal with the mysticism of letters before he has fulfilled the required preconditions necessary for success.

This clearly shows how irresponsible it is when writings of Oriental origin are interpreted incorrectly and translated literally into an intellectual language.

The true Kabbalistic mysticism of letters, as described in this book, is ancient and founded on the analogies of universal laws. The universal Kabbalistic mysticism is something quite different from mere exercises in the transfer of one's consciousness, and it does not matter if you use only single letters or more extensive mantras. When working practically, one has to take into consideration the universal laws and their analogies in one's spirit, soul and body. In true Kabbalistic mysticism the Kabbalist not only operates with his consciousness alone, but learns to apply letters practically, and at a later stage compound words or formulas as well, with the four basic attributes of his spirit — will, intellect, feeling and consciousness (imagination). The actual purpose of the true Kabbalah, of true Kabbalistic mysticism, is of course that these four basic attributes of the spirit first be kept separate and later united by the Kabbalist, thus enabling him to project a letter with its powers and analogies practically into the spheres of the spirit, the soul and physical matter within himself and outside himself, using all four basic attributes of the spirit.

In the practical part of this book, the aspiring Kabbalist will be given the details of this mysticism in a systematic course consisting of various stages, along with details on the use of the tetrapolar magnet in the spirit, soul and body.

Kabbalistic Magic

Before concluding the theoretical description of Kabbalistic mysticism and proceeding to describe the practical Kabbalah, I would like to make a few brief remarks on Kabbalistic magic so that the Kabbalist can assess this correctly, too.

Summing up what has been said, it is the aim of Kabbalistic mysticism to prepare the microcosm, the body, soul and spirit, for the application of the letters so that the Kabbalist will be able to serve the Creator, which means to act creatively through the Word. On the basis of systematic exercises aided by the will, intellect, feeling and consciousness, together with imagination, each letter takes on a significance quite different than when it is pronounced merely intellectually. Words composed in a Kabbalistic manner in exact accordance with the universal laws are words of creation which have the same effect as the ones pronounced by God Himself.

To speak Kabbalistically means to create something out of nothing. This is the greatest mystery which can ever be revealed to and understood by a human being, who, like God, is consciously capable of setting the universal laws in motion. Each word which is uttered in the correct magico-Kabbalistic manner must become reality at once. Never will one who is uninitiated succeed in releasing the power of the letters tetrapolarly, for he will not possess the abilities of the spirit, soul and body to creatively utter Kabbalistic letters.

Mere theoretical knowledge alone cannot enable anyone to set into motion the powers which are contained in the individual letters and words. Therefore I have repeatedly recommended working practically through my first book, *Initiation into Hermetics*. A certain level of maturity is attained by gradually training the body, soul and spirit; and on the way to perfection, the four fundamental attributes of the spirit are trained accordingly in the preparatory exercises.

Anyone who begins immediately with Kabbalistic mysticism without having completed the first course will have to develop each fundamental attribute gradually by very extensive exercises. This is much more difficult than practicing and completing the exercises in my first book.

Kabbalistic mysticism prepares the body, soul and spirit to learn and make practical use of the magic Word, the cosmic language. Kabbalistic magic can only be implemented if body, soul and spirit have been prepared accordingly, conforming with the universal laws, the Tetragrammaton key.

Hindu terminology has chosen the word *vag* to denote Kabbalistic magic. This word indicates the state of maturity of the Vishuddha Chakra, which is situated in the larynx. The difference between a magician and a Kabbalist is that, for the all the effects he achieves, the magician is indebted to the spiritual beings which cause the desired effects. The magician who is knowledgeable in Kabbalah, the true Kabbalist, causes all the effects with his creative word, irrespective of the sphere or plane, without needing the help of any entity.

There are many systems of Kabbalistic magic, and many keys can be used in practice. To describe them all would fill volumes. Just think: if, for instance, one considers that a basic attribute of the spirit may be achieved with the help of thirty-two different systems, and since the human spirit possesses four fundamental attributes, this already results in 128 systems which would have to be divided into ten stages each in accordance with the Sephirothic scale of keys.

I am going to describe the systematic use of only one key, namely the Tetragrammaton key, the key of absoluteness and realization. In Kabbalistic magic the Tetragrammaton key is one of the most important universal keys, with the help of which the study of Kabbalah is started everywhere. It is reserved to Divine Providence alone to decide whether I shall be allowed to systematically publish any further keys relating to the micro- and macrocosm. This, of course, depends above all on how much longer I remain on this planet. With this book I will initiate the Kabbalist into the mysteries of the unutterable name, that is, into the use of the Tetragrammaton key, to the point where he will be enabled to make use of the universal language and act creatively through the Word.

Finally, in this chapter I shall mention the talismans of Kabbalistic magic. Magico-Kabbalistic talismans are either signs, symbols or letters, engraved or written in analogy to the universal laws. The individual letter or sign is charged with the help of the creative Word, or, speaking in a strictly Kabbalistic sense, by means of the four fundamental attributes of the spirit. A magico-Kabbalistic talisman of this kind will never fail to produce its effect, since the Kabbalistic word is banished into the respective seal, talisman or pentacle, etc., for the purpose of becoming effective, and therefore represents a true magic tool. Of course, only an experienced magician, one who is an expert in magic and Kabbalah, may occupy himself with magico-Kabbalistic talismanology.

PART II

PRACTICE

Practice

Even in the theoretical section of this book, the attentive reader has been given views regarding Kabbalistic mysticism which are different than those contained in any other book on the subject. Kabbalistic mysticism is the most difficult subject to be learned in Hermetic science, for it requires not only knowledge but practical experience and cognition as well. Therefore, much will remain incomprehensible to the person who reads my book just to study its contents theoretically, for he will lack the necessary practical prerequisites. This is why I have pointed out, at the beginning of this book, that it is absolutely necessary to have practiced and completed at least the first eight steps of my initial volume, *Initiation into Hermetics,* in order to be able to attain satisfactory results in Kabbalistic mysticism. Having gradually trained his spirit, soul and body tetrapolarly, the student has been given — apart from many magical powers and abilities — a high degree of intuition by the Akasha principle.

Consequently, he will not only be able to comprehend the profundity of the universal laws, and thus also of Kabbalah, but he will be able to apply the Kabbalah practically as well. Without tetrapolar exercises of spirit, soul and body, it will be impossible to master the Kabbalistic or universal language. To speak Kabbalistically does not mean speaking with one's mouth or intellect, but to have a tetrapolar mode of expression. And the ability to express oneself in a tetrapolar fashion may well be called the "true Kabbalah."

If someone studies Kabbalistic science simply from an

intellectual point of view, he will never be able to get the right idea of it, and even less will he be able to make practical use of it. The aspiring Kabbalist must learn to speak, almost like a little child, by gradually acquiring the tetrapolar use of a Kabbalistic letter, and later of a Kabbalistic word, sentence, and so on. To occupy oneself immediately with the Kabbalah without having undergone previous magical schooling would necessitate a gradual development of the tetrapolar prerequisites of spirit and soul necessary for the utterance of the Kabbalah. This, however, would mean a tremendous loss of time and would require great effort, as any reasonable person must admit. Therefore, no one should begin the practice of Kabbalistic mysticism unless he has thoroughly practiced the instructions given concerning the first Tarot card, i.e. in *Initiation into Hermetics*.

Those who have practiced and mastered the steps described in my first book will soon enjoy good results in the Kabbalistic science. But whosoever, out of mere curiosity or imprudence, immediately advances to the methods which describe the use of the true Kabbalistic mysticism without having previously attained a magical equilibrium will subject himself to various dangers. For in practice he will come into contact with various powers which he will be unable to control and which will be harmful to his health. Therefore, anyone who is not sufficiently prepared for this path is hereby warned. People of high moral and ethical standards with noble qualities of spirit and soul may engage in practical Kabbalah, but like anybody else they will have to acquire the necessary abilities.

The teaching method of Kabbalistic mysticism involves the use of letters in order to speak and be effective Kabbalistically, i.e., creatively. Just as the visual, acoustical and intuitional exercises in *Initiation into Hermetics* contributed to the spirit's development, the aspiring Kabbalist must now practice the individual letters — first visually, later acoustically, and finally intuitively —

in order to be able to pronounce a letter Kabbalistically with complete consciousness. Therefore, the first step involves the visual practice of pronouncing a letter. The visual aspect of a letter refers to its light and color in relation to the eyes, and is analogous to the principle of the will. Thus the student once again begins with the first characteristic of the spirit, the principle of the will.

Before describing the exercises with the individual letters, it is my intention to describe the practice of the universal Kabbalah and to note that I cannot acknowledge the claims of any specific world religion to be the original source of this high science. To practically study the true Kabbalah, the aspiring Kabbalist need not have a knowledge of Oriental languages, Hebrew, or any other tongue. The universal expression of a letter is not its form but its color or, to be more exact, its color-vibration. Since the color-vibration of a letter is its most visible form of expression, anyone can engage in the Kabbalah, regardless of the intellectual language he speaks. An Occidental is just as capable of imagining a letter's proper color as is an Oriental. To imagine a letter in its true color means, at the same time, to pronounce it with a certain vibration of light in the mental world, the mental sphere.

In this regard, one might object that there are different hues of color, and allege that color cannot therefore be the most appropriate form of expressing a letter. Objections like these, however, will only be made by non-initiates, for an initiate knows very well that the color a person imagines will depend upon his maturity. Depending on your individual voice, you may pronounce an A with a higher or lower tone of voice, thus producing a personal sound-vibration which is different from anyone else's; but in reality you are simply pronouncing an A, which will be perceived as an A by anyone who hears it. The same is true of color: whether you imagine a darker or lighter color-vibration is not so important; the basic tone of the color-vibration always plays the key role and will denote the respective letter. Though it is possible to record color-vibrations with physical instrumentation, it must be stressed that the human eye's susceptibility to color depends on a person's individual sensitivity. Thus the above objection is not applicable, for the aspiring Kabbalist will pronounce each letter, accompanied by its respective color, in accordance with his own individuality, i.e., his own plastic imaginative abilities. Since he has practiced the principle of the will, he will be able to transfer the power that is due the respective letter into color-vibrations. The exercises in the first step of this course in Kabbalistic instruction consist of learning how to express the whole alphabet by colors.

Step I
The Mysticism of Letters

I begin the first step with exercises involving the Latin rather than the Hebrew alphabet for Kabbalistic use, starting with the first letter. The Kabbalist will practice the letter A either seated in an asana[2] position or standing up. The color-vibration of the letter A is light blue. The actual practice is completely individual and — as just mentioned — may be carried out either by assuming the asana position or by standing up.

In your mind, pronounce the letter A, but draw it out, at the same time imagining that, as you pronounce it in the spirit, it assumes a light blue color, and that the entire room takes on this light blue color. After some practice you will not only fill the whole training room with this mental A (whose light blue coloration must resemble a light), but the whole universe as well.

Since he has learned to work with the elements and with light, the experienced magician will not find this exercise difficult. When, by this exercise, you have attained such proficiency that a light blue color immediately fills the whole universe whenever you spiritually pronounce the letter A, you may proceed to the next exercise. This consists of uttering the light blue A into your body or microcosm and, with it, filling up your whole body, which you must regard as a hollow space. Having achieved proficiency in this, you will next learn to pronounce the letter A in your mind, silently, though as if you were uttering it through your mouth. Then you will learn to do the opposite: perceive the whole universe as a light blue letter A which you inhale or absorb into your body or microcosm as if it were a hollow space.

---

[2]This position is described in Step II of *Initiation Into Hermetics,* and is not to be interpreted as the yogic position.

You must become very familiar with this deductive and inductive way of speaking with your mouth and your whole body. In these exercises, never pronounce the letter physically; the entire process takes place in your spirit, that is, in your mind alone. As soon as you have sufficient practice in this, you will proceed, with the letter A, to accumulate light within yourself and then dissolve it into the universe, similar to the process I have described in *Initiation into Hermetics*. In this present exercise, you must learn to pronounce a letter (in this case A) spiritually, simultaneously giving it a specific shape. In so doing, you may imagine the whole universe filled with a light blue color. While you are pronouncing the letter A, the light blue color will condense in size and form to the shape you want it to have.

In this process of imagining in three dimensions, one may first mentally imagine the letter A several times, and with every repetition intensify the imagined plastic color until the desired shape is attained. The shape itself is less important than the imagination and desire — it is entirely up to the student as to whether he chooses to condense the light blue color into a ball, a flame, a small cloud or any other shape.

At any rate, you must learn to condense the letter in its relevant color by using your imaginal power of plasticizing in the microcosm as well as the macrocosm, and then dissolve it again later. By this process of condensation you will learn to give the letter its appropriate dynamics and power of expansion. When the Kabbalist learns how to make a formula work dynamically, he will realize how important this is.

If the Kabbalist masters the exercises with the letter A perfectly in the manner described, let him continue on with the same exercises with the second and each subsequent letter. The exercise is always the same, so I will not repeat it, but simply give the color-vibration that is to be used in the practice of each letter.

The Kabbalist shall imagine the second letter, B, in a

wonderful light violet color, and shall perform the same exercises as with the letter A, i.e.:

* in the exercise room
* in the whole universe
* in the body as inner hollow space
* inductively and deductively, i.e., materializing and dematerializing the letter.

The third letter is C and must be practiced in a vermilion color-vibration.

The fourth letter, D, must be practiced in dark blue color-vibration. The Kabbalist will realize that these exercises become easier the more often he repeats them, and will have no difficulty at all in performing the exercises with all the letters; he need only change the color with each letter.

E is the fifth letter. It is expressed by dark violet.

The sixth letter, F, is to be practiced in light green. F vibrates in the cosmos in light green and must always be differentiated from:

G, the seventh letter of the alphabet, which is practiced in a grass-green color.

The eighth letter is H. It must be practiced in a silver-violet color. You must not confound it with the letter B, which must have a light violet color, whereas the H is to be practiced in a somewhat darker shade of violet with a silvery glitter. The same applies to the CH.

The ninth letter is I, the cosmic color of which is light opal. Opal colors have hues of green, red, blue and violet, that is, they have a spectrum of light. Every Kabbalist should firmly commit this complex of colors to his memory, so as to be able to work more easily with the letter I. Since opal represents nearly all colors, in the Hebrew Kabbalah the I or Jod is regarded as the first letter, the one from which all the others are derived.

J, the tenth letter, also has an opal color-vibration which is, however, somewhat darker; the difference in color between the I and the J is easily recognizable.

In the eleventh place is the K, which has to be imagined in silvery blue.

The twelfth letter, the L, is to be practiced in a dark green light-vibration. The dark green of this letter is a lush green which is reminiscent of the green of an olive.

The M is letter number thirteen, with a blue-green color-vibration. The blue-green of M is reminiscent of the color of the sea, and it is not without good reason that M is attributed to the Water principle in the analogy of the four elements.

N, being the fourteenth letter, is to be practiced in a meat-red color-vibration.

The color-vibration of O, the fifteenth letter, is a dark ultra-marine.

P, the sixteenth letter, has a dark grey color-vibration.

In Kabbalah, the seventeenth letter, the Q, is not regarded as an independent letter, but as a combination of K and W. There-fore, Q is not to be practiced.

The eighteenth letter of our alphabet is the R, which the Kabbalist must imagine in a golden color, shining wonderfully.

The S is the nineteenth letter. It is to be practiced in a purple-red color until it is mastered perfectly.

The SCH or SH, the twentieth letter, is a combined letter as far as spelling is concerned, but it plays an important role in the Kabbalistic language. SCH has a fiery red color-vibration and is attributed to the pure Fire element in Kabbalah.

The twenty-first letter, T, is to be practiced in brown-black.

Letter number twenty-two, the U, is practiced in velvet-black, but the black must be perceived as color and not as emptiness.

The twenty-third letter, the V, is a variation of the letter F, and therefore it is also practiced in light green.

W, the twenty-fourth letter, must be practiced in a lilac color-vibration. V is merely a phonetic variation of W and not an independent letter from the Kabbalistic point of view.

The same is true of X, the twenty-fifth letter, for it is composed of K and S and not regarded as a single letter from the Kabbalistic point of view.

The Y or Ü, the twenty-sixth letter, is to be practiced in a pink color-vibration.

Z is regarded as the last letter of the alphabet and is to be practiced in a lemon-yellow or light yellow color-vibration.

Finally, something must be said about the umlaut. The Ö is to be practiced in dark orange, and the Ä in a light brown hue (the color of loam).

When the Kabbalist has worked his way through all the letters in the manner described, and is able to call forth each letter he pronounces in his spirit in its respective color-vibration, he may proceed with the next exercises.

As soon as the student of the Kabbalah has gone through all the letters in their respective colors, and has achieved enough proficiency, both inductively and deductively, to project them from his body into the universe and, vice versa, to draw them from the universe back into his body and condense them, he may continue as follows: He shall conduct the letters, in the same way, into the different regions of his body, taking into consideration their analogous relationship to the elements.

The student once again begins with the letter A, which pertains to the element of Air, and conducts it into the Air region of the body, i.e, into the chest, where he pronounces it mentally and imagines it to be there in a light blue color. Having retained the light blue color in his chest imaginally for a longer period of time, he may dissolve it again with his imagination. He must have the feeling that the light-vibration of blue has completely disappeared from his chest.

In the next exercise, he mentally begins to pronounce the A and to call forth the light blue light-vibration in his chest. Whenever pronouncing the A in his mind, the light-vibration of blue will be condensed in his chest. However, this condensation should not influence the color. The power of expansion must be retained in the chest and increased from exercise to exercise. Of course, none of these exercises should affect his breathing; they should not mislead the student into holding his breath at the moment of accumulation. To succumb to this temptation will only overcome the student at the very beginning. Later, when he is accustomed to calling forth dynamics of whatever type, whether internally or externally, blockages such as irregular breathing, undesirable muscle tension, and so on, will no longer occur. After having condensed the A in its light blue color to the point where he resembles an overinflated tire, he makes it dissolve again in the universe by pronouncing it.

In a further exercise, the student imaginally expands the cosmic A, in its light blue color, into the whole universe, and tries to get it into the region of his chest by inhaling it in through his mouth or nose. A few quiet breaths will suffice, and the student will have filled his chest with the light blue light-vibration. When inhaling the color-vibration of the letter A, one must breathe with regularity, without any special effort and without holding one's breath. Also, deep breathing must be avoided, for the student will find this disturbing later on.

After achieving success with these exercises, the student no longer needs to draw in the light blue light-vibrations through the mouth or nose when speaking the letter A in the innermost of his chest; instead, he can now draw them in through the periphery of the chest, as in the exercise dealing with pore-breathing. Also in this case, the student must try to achieve sufficient dynamics by repeatedly using his powers of imagination. In short, he must be capable of drawing any letter vibration into the respective region of the body and emitting it again, inductively and deductively, in a simple or condensed state. These exercises must be repeated until the student achieves such proficiency that he can perform all the Kabbalistic tasks mentioned so far with effortless ease.

The umlaut Ä with its loamy-brown light-coloration pertains to the Earth element and is to be practiced until it is mastered completely in the Earth region of the body, which begins at the coccyx and expands over the thighs down to the soles of the feet.

The letter B, with its light violet light-vibration, is analogous to the Water element, which influences the whole region of the abdomen. The exercises are the same as those described for the letter A concerning the region of the chest, and must be repeated until mastered perfectly.

The C with its vermilion light-vibration is subject to the Fire element and pertains to the head. It has to be practiced in the same way as letter A.

I may point out once more that the student must dynamically charge the relevant region of his body with the respective color-vibration and later dissolve it again into the universe. If he omits the dissolution, he will cause a disturbance in the harmony of the elements in his microcosm; hence the dynamics, the power of expansion, may have discordant effects on him, which in turn may have detrimental consequences not only for his mental and astral but even for his material existence. He may not become ill right away, but he will certainly get the feeling of disharmony. This remark is to warn and, at the same time, to encourage the student always to perform his exercises conscientiously. The aspiring Kabbalist is dealing with powers whose full scope he will learn to know at a later date.

The next letter to be practiced is D, with its dark blue color-vibration. D is subject to the Earth element and has to be practiced like the umlaut Ä, from the coccyx down to the soles of the feet.

The E with its dark violet light-vibration is analogous to the Fire element and therefore has to be practiced (like C) in the Fire region, in the entire head.

Now follows the letter F with a light green color-vibration. Since it pertains to the Water element, it is practiced, like B, in the Water region, the entire abdomen.

G vibrates in a grass-green color and belongs to the Earth element. Like Ä and D, it is therefore practiced in the described manner in the Earth region of one's own microcosm, from the coccyx to the soles of the feet.

The difference between F and G is that F is light green, one should almost say yellowish-green, whereas G is a grass-green, a lush green color-light-vibration. At all events, the student must be able to tell the F from the G at once by the different color-vibrations.

The H with its silver-violet light-vibration corresponds to the element of Water and is therefore practiced in the abdominal region, like B and F.

The CH has a violet color-vibration and thus pertains to the Akasha principle and is to be practiced in the region between the abdomen and chest, in the solar plexus. This region is also called the "golden section" and forms a kind of intermediate region.

The student imagines the letter I in an opalescent light-color-vibration in which the lighter colors are dominant. The I pertains to the Earth element and, like Ä, D and G, therefore belongs to the Earth region from the coccyx to the soles of the feet, but it is to be especially practiced in both feet.

J has an opalescent color-vibration, similar to that of I; its hues, however, are somewhat darker. The J, too, pertains to the Earth element and therefore to the Earth region of the microcosm, where the exercises with this letter are to take place.

The letter K has a silver-blue color-light-vibration and is controlled by two elements, namely Fire and Air, rather than by one pure element alone. The relevant regions of the body are the head and the chest. Exercises with K must therefore be done in both of these regions.

Now follows the letter L, which has a dark green, let us say olive-green, color-light-vibration. It pertains to the Air element and thus belongs to the Air region, like A and K; that is, it is to be practiced in the chest area.

Continuing in alphabetical sequence, the exercises with M, which must have a blue-green light-vibration analogous to the Water element, come next. Like B, F and H, the M has to be practiced in the Water region of the body, namely the abdominal region.

Then follows N in a dark red color-light-vibration. The N is subject to the Fire element and, like C, E and K, must be practiced in the head until mastered perfectly.

The letter O with its ultramarine-colored light-vibration also pertains to the Fire element and is practiced in the head like C, E, K and N. Its ultramarine color must be absolutely distinguished from light blue and dark blue.

The Ö is the second umlaut and has a dark orange light-coloration. It is subject to the Fire element and is practiced in the Fire region, in the head, like C, E, K, N and O.

The next letter in the alphabet is P, which has a dark grey color-light-vibration and pertains to the Earth element. Like the letters Ä, D, G, I and J, P is to be practiced in the Earth region, in both legs starting from the thighs down to the soles of the feet.

The R with its gold-colored light-vibration must first be

practiced in the Akasha principle, the intermediate region of the solar plexus, and, after this has been mastered perfectly, in the Water region or abdomen, like the letters B, F, H and M.

S with its purple light-vibration belongs to the Fire element and must therefore be practiced in the Fire region, the head, like the letters C, E, K, N, O and Ö.

SCH has a fire-red light-vibration and is subject to the Fire element. Like the S, it is to be practiced in the head. There is a difference between S and SCH in color. The S has a purple color coming very near to brick red, whereas SCH has a blazing red, or glowing red, shade. In the *Sepher Yetzirah,* SCH is attributed to the pure Fire element. The Akasha principle, that is, God in His creative aspect, created the Fire element by this letter.

The following letter, the T, has to be practiced in a brown-black light-vibration. T pertains to the Earth element and must therefore be practiced in the Earth region of the microcosm, in both legs, like Ä, D, G, I, J and P.

Next in this series is the letter U with its shining black, velvet-black, light-vibration. The location of its exercises is first in the intermediate region or solar plexus. After completing the exercises in this Akasha region, the letter U must be practiced in the Earth region, like Ä, D, G, I, J, P and T.

W with its lilac light-vibration is subject to the Akasha principle as well as to the Air principle. Therefore this letter is to be practiced first in the Akasha region, the intermediate region of the solar plexus, and, after having learned to master this, in the Air region, the chest, like A, K and L.

The Y stands also for the umlaut Ü in Kabbalistic pronunciation and is practiced in a pink-colored light-vibration in the Fire region, the head, like C, E, K, N, O, Ö, S and SCH, since it is subject to the Fire element.

The last letter of the alphabet, the Z, has a light yellow or lemon-yellow light-vibration. It is controlled by the Air element and must therefore be practiced in the Air region, the chest, and is to be practiced like A, K, L, and W. The Z must not be confused with C, which has a vermilion light-vibration and which is spoken sharply. Z, with its light yellow or lemon-yellow light-vibration, has to be pronounced with a humming, a soft voice, similar to S.

Having completed all the exercises described here with each letter of the alphabet, the student of Kabbalah has concluded one full stage in Kabbalistic practice and may pass on to the following exercises. It is a prerequisite that the student should have at least some fundamental knowledge of human anatomy. If he does not, he must learn. He may gain this knowledge from any anatomy textbook. It would be ridiculous if a student of Kabbalistic mysticism did not know where the liver, kidneys, and so forth were to be found in the human body.

In the exercises that follow, occult anatomy is taken into consideration. The procedure is the same as with the exercises which place each letter in the physical region of its corresponding element. If the student of the Kabbalah were to attempt these next exercises without being able to transfer his consciousness into the physical organ with which he is practicing, his efforts would be unsuccessful. Therefore, the Kabbalist will find it justifiable that I make mention of my first book, *Initiation into Hermetics*, a course of instruction in which one is taught how to transfer his consciousness; and therefore it will not be difficult for him now to deal with the individual organs Kabbalistically.

Anyone who wants to follow the path of Kabbalistic mysticism, but who lacks the proper preparation, must practice the transfer of his consciousness before taking up any Kabbalistic exercises. Otherwise he will never succeed in mastering the visionary Kabbalistic exercises which lead to activity of the principle of the will in the microcosm and macrocosm.

The second and last stage of the first step deals with this practical activity, i.e., the use of the letters in each organ, which must then be stimulated and brought under control in analogy with the universal laws. The exercise is as follows:

Begin again with the first letter of the alphabet, the letter A, which is now to be practiced not in the entire chest but exclusively in the lungs. The student transfers himself with his whole consciousness into each lobe of the lungs and feels and perceives like a lung and does his exercises there. The A in its light blue color is again inhaled imaginally from the whole universe into each lobe of the lungs and later dissolved back into the universe. If the experiment is successful, the dynamics of this exercise will also be formed by condensation of the light blue light-color-vibration, first by inhaling through the mouth or nose and later by imaginal breathing through the pores. One may not pass on to the second or any subsequent letter until the A has been thoroughly mastered in the lobes of the lungs in the manner described.

The next letter is umlaut Ä, which is to be practiced in the same way as the A, but with a loamy-brown light-color-vibration and in the anus.

B, in its light violet color-vibration, is to be practiced in the entire eyeball of the right eye.

C, in a vermilion color-vibration, is to be practiced in the stomach.

The exercises with the letter D take place in the right ear in a dark blue color-vibration.

Exercises in the ear do not merely extend over the auricle, but the whole auditory organ.

E, in a dark violet (Akashic violet) light-vibration is practiced in the entire spine, from the coccyx upwards to the back of the head.

F, with its light green color-vibration, is practiced in the left hand.

G has a grass-green (lush green) color-light-vibration and is practiced in all the phases of the left eye.

H, with a silvery-violet light-color-vibration, is to be practiced in the whole right arm, from the shoulder down to the finger tips.

Now follows the letter CH, with whose violet light-color-vibration the exercises must be carried out so as to stimulate, and place under one's control, the whole left leg from the thigh down to the tips of the toes.

The location of the exercises with the letter I and its light opalescent color-light-vibration is in the left kidney, into which one's consciousness must be transferred.

It is more difficult with the letter J and its dark opalescent light coloration, which must be practiced in the diaphragm. The diaphragm consists of a muscular, membranous partition (thin-walled tissue) into which the student of Kabbalah must transfer his consciousness in order to stimulate it. He should not pass on to the next letter until he is certain that he has mastered the exercises in the diaphragm.

K, with its silvery-blue light-color-vibration, is practiced in the left ear. Since the student is already experienced in this, having learned to stimulate his right ear with the letter D, it will not be difficult for him to stimulate his left ear as well.

In order to stimulate the spleen, the letter L is practiced with a dark green light-color-vibration.

The location of the exercises with the letter M, in a blue-green light-vibration, is in the cavity of the abdomen, but under no circumstances in the intestines. To make the exercises with the M easier for him, the student must imagine the abdomen as a hollow space void of intestines or any other organs. With an appropriate attitude and transfer of consciousness, he will fully succeed in stimulating the inner cavity of the abdomen without considering any other organs such as the bowels, gallbladder, etc.

The next letter to be practiced is the N with its dark red color-light-vibration. The liver is stimulated with N after having transferred one's consciousness into it.

The throat is the location of the exercises with the letter O and its ultramarine light-vibration. From a Kabbalistic point of view, the pharynx includes the entire throat and the windpipe.

Umlaut Ö, in a dark orange light-coloration, is to be practiced like all the other letters, its location being in the testicles of men and the ovaries of women. It rests with the student either to stimulate one testicle alone or both testicles at the same time. With regard to the female genitals, however, it would appear to be advantageous to stimulate and master the left ovary first and then the right one.

P is practiced in a dark green light-color-vibration in the right nostril.

The left nostril is reserved for exercises with the letter R, in a golden light-color-vibration.

Now follows the letter S in a purple light-color-vibration. It is to be practiced in the gallbladder.

With the letter SCH — a fire-red light-color-vibration — the brain is stimulated, the cerebellum as well as the cerebrum, which means the whole inside of the head.

The right kidney is worked at by the letter T, in a brownish-black light-color-vibration.

The letter U, with its velvet-black, or shining black, light-vibration, is for stimulating the pancreas, situated in the solar plexus.

Using the lilac-colored light-vibration of the W, the student must stimulate the entire intestine, from the duodenum to the colon and right down to the rectum.

The letter Y or umlaut Ü is to be practiced in a pink-colored light-vibration in the heart.

Finally, the last letter of the alphabet, the Z, with its light yellow color-vibration, is also to be practiced in the heart.

In this way, the student of Kabbalah has gone through the entire alphabet with its analogies to the human body, and has learned, in practice, to transfer his consciousness into any organ of his body, and to be active there in a magico-Kabbalistic manner. Through these exercises, the Kabbalist attains the ability to know, stimulate and master any organ in the body, his own or anyone else's.

The exercises in transferring one's consciousness into each organ usually cause more blood to accumulate in the organ concerned, which is generally sensed as warmth, sometimes even as heat, since, by transferring his consciousness into the organ, the Kabbalist's complete attention is dedicated to it. The blood profusion sensed as warmth is erroneously regarded by many mystics as a certain divine power; however, it has nothing to do with this, and is merely a physiological and psychological effect. The Kabbalist should not pay any special attention to this accumulation of blood, and should regard the warmth as a natural side effect of his exercises. The expansiveness of the accumulated powers in the organs will not do him any harm; it will be completely innocuous. After all, the Kabbalist has learned to cause condensations or accumulations of the various types — electrical and magnetic, with elements and with light — so that his body already possesses a certain degree of elasticity and resistance due to these individual powers. Anyone to whom this applies may do all the exercises described so far without harm. He will even regard them as a blessing in every respect.

The student may ask why the exercises are not carried out sequentially in the body, in one organ after the other from head to foot or vice versa. The answer is that it is more advantageous for the practicing Kabbalist to follow the sequence of the letters, and thus skip from one organ to the other, avoiding an over-accumulation of blood in the organs of his body.

By going from one organ to another, for instance to an opposite one, the feeling of blood accumulation will drop in the organ which was practiced earlier. It may happen now and again that by transferring one's consciousness into a certain organ and by stimulating it, there arises a feeling of pain quite apart from the sensation of warmth. This would be a signal that the respective organ or part of the body is either over-sensitive or else diseased, even though there are no visible symptoms and the disease is otherwise undetectable. In such a case, and before proceeding any further, the Kabbalist, using the power of his imagination, should repeatedly effect an accumulation of light energy in the diseased organ for a complete recovery. With the help of his powers of imagination, the diseased organ will be healed by this repeated accumulation of light-energy in such a way that the Kabbalist may then carry on with his exercises there.

A second question may arise: namely, what must be done in cases where an organ has been removed by surgery? In such a case only the mortal frame, the material form, has been removed, but the astral function of the organ continues to exist, and the student must stimulate the organ in the same way as if it were still physically present. When doing the exercises, he simply imagines the organ to be where it ought to be. People who have had an arm or leg amputated sometimes experience the same pains as if they still possessed the physical limb. Physiologists call this sensation of physical pain in amputated places "subjective overstrain of the nerve cord." The Hermeticist knows, however, that in the astral world the missing physical organ still exists in its astral shape.

It may well be that some readers who are engaged in astrology may take offense at the fact that the color-light-vibrations of each letter as described here do not always agree with the common astrological attributions. I reject such a criticism on the grounds that Kabbalistic mysticism has nothing to do with mantic astrology.

All the Kabbalistic exercises of Step I in this book will strengthen the principle of the will in the Kabbalistic mystic to the highest degree. Furthermore, they will allow him to acquire the ability to use the letters and their color-vibrations Kabbalistically in the microcosm and macrocosm, this being the actual purpose of all the exercises in Step I.

Step II
Kabbalistic Incantation

In Step I of this course in Kabbalistic mysticism, the student has learned to pronounce each letter by way of its corresponding color, both inductively and deductively, in his own body, the microcosm, as well as in the universe, the macrocosm. He will now learn to give each letter any shape he likes, and to pronounce it in the language of colors in the same way, i.e., to charge any object with the respective letter vibration. Even now he will be able to imagine — even if not yet quite clearly — the scope of effects on the body, soul and spirit when he has learned to pronounce each letter tetrapolarly.

This method of using words so as to make them magically and dynamically effective can only be taught to a student by a true initiate. The student will now realize that everything he has had to learn, with great effort, up to now has been absolutely necessary for:

* learning the use of the cosmic language; and
* attaining the ability to actually speak tetrapolarly later on.

Upon completion of Step II of this course, the student will have taken a further step forward, for in learning the cosmic language he will have to make use of the second aspect of his personality, his intellectual part or Air principle, and use the letters together with sounds. The letters come to life with sound, and it will be the student's next task to use or pronounce each letter with the tone analogous to it.

The technique is exactly the same as with the visionary exercises involving the light-color-vibrations, the only difference being that rather than each letter having its own specific note, one and the same note is repeated with a number of different letters. Only in connection with the light- color-vibration does each letter receive its correspondent sound-vibration. In the following letter exercises with tones, the color-light is to be brought into harmony with the sound vibration in order to be able to express the letter more fully. The exercises with sound-vibrations, in connection with color-light-vibrations, must also be carried out inductively and deductively in the micro- and the macrocosm.

Let the student begin with the exercises in his whole body, then in the individual regions of the elements, and finally in the individual organs of the body, proceeding in the same way as he did with the individual letters with their color-light-vibrations.

In his body, which he must consider as a hollow space, the student imagines the light blue color while simultaneously repeating in his mind the letter A several times on the pitch of the note G (G-major). It is quite up to him whether to work with all the letters in alphabetical order, inductively and deductively in his whole body, then in each region of the elements and finally in each organ of his body, or to choose the second possibility — to work Kabbalistically with each letter, first in the whole body, then in its respective region of the elements, and finally in the respective organ of the body. It is the aim of all the exercises of Step II to connect the intellectual aspect, the Air principle, with the color principle and the respective sound-vibrations.

The list below shows the student the sound pitch of the letters he must work with:

letter	vibrates in	tone
A		G
Ä (AE)		C
B		A

C	D
D	C
E	D
F	F#
G	F
H	A
CH	D#
I	G
J	G#
K	B
L	F
M	D
N	A
O	C
Ö (OE)	D#
P	B
R	C
S	G#
SCH (SH)	C
T	F
U	B
W	G
Ü (UE) & Y	C#
Z	G

It is not necessary for the student practicing these sound combinations to be musically gifted. It will be sufficient if he has some kind of musical instrument, or at least a tuning fork, to identify the proper pitch. If necessary, it may also suffice if the student simply hums the scale of notes to find the pitch of the respective sound. The reproduction of sound need not be so exact, for not everybody is musically gifted. The main thing in the application of sound is to call forth the letter in the relevant light-vibration and sound-vibration.

Later on, it will become quite clear to the student (and he will appreciate the fact) that the sound-vibration of each letter pronounced in his mind (i.e., in his thoughts) causes a special effect in the mental world; furthermore, that sound and color-vibration, when applied together and pronounced as a letter in a low undertone, have their influence on the astral senses or astral body and, when pronounced aloud, have their effect on the material world or physical body. This recognition will be of great advantage to the Kabbalist at a later time, when he endeavors to cause certain effects either in the mental, astral or material world.

If the student has conscientiously gone through the entire alphabet in all phases and thus has completely mastered each letter:

1. in the whole body
2. in the regions of the elements, and
3. in each organ of the body,

and can repeat these tasks effortlessly at any time, he may regard the exercises of Step II as completed. It is not recommended that he perform these exercises in haste, for conscientiousness is very important here, and the greater the student's perseverance in his work, the greater will be the success which will crown his diligence.

By following the exercises indicated here, the student of the Kabbalah will not only learn to use the powers but, in accordance with the universal laws of analogy, will make his spirit, soul and body resistant and elastic and will be spared from various influences — which is absolutely necessary when working with Kabbalah, the magic of words. The student who has prepared his body, soul and spirit Kabbalistically will never be influenced by any entities of any kind whatsoever, and will be able to contact other beings, whether positive or negative, without a circle and without any other means of protection. Also, when applying certain formulas which release certain powers into the universe, the Kabbalist will always remain protected from any possible harmful influences, providing his soul and spirit have been prepared accordingly.

Therefore, the student should not proceed any further until he has conscientiously completed these exercises. Furthermore, he must differentiate between the customary intellectual and the cosmic language and, when doing his exercises, must always remember to work Kabbalistically. Being constantly aware of this, the sounds, colors and other analogies will never enter his consciousness when he employs his normal speech. Therefore, the Kabbalist must never confuse normal and Kabbalistic language, nor connect the two.

Step III
Aqua Vitae Kabbalisticae

In the two preceding steps the Kabbalist has learned how to pronounce each letter Kabbalistically, in the proper order:

* in their color-vibration, by the principle of the will which is subject to the Fire element, and
* to pronounce the letter Kabbalistically, in the vibration of the Air principle, and to dynamize each letter in bipolar fashion.

The inductive and deductive procedures enable the Kabbalist to apply the vibrations of a letter in any place, whether inside himself or, outside himself, in the universe. By learning how to condense the power of expansion gradually, he attains the necessary resistance and tenacity to remain steadfast and to withstand these vibrations. That this ability is of great importance from the Hermetic point of view will be quite clear to any Kabbalist who has come this far.

Now I am going to introduce the student of the Kabbalah to a third vibration of the letters, which he must also learn to master by doing suitable exercises. In this third type of vibration, the elemental attribute of the letter, which the Kabbalist has to acquire intuitively, is of great importance. Every letter has one, sometimes even two, element vibrations.

Begin again with the letter A. The Kabbalist mentally utters the A into his body, imagining it to be a hollow space. In doing this, he must have a feeling of lightness. As soon as he has succeeded, after practice, in accomplishing this a few times, and as soon as he genuinely feels this lightness whenever he gives utterance in his mind, he may eventually pronounce the A in a low voice and imagine that the A vibration also calls forth this feeling of lightness in his workroom. After a number of successful attempts, he extends his exercises by transferring the feeling of lightness to the whole universe.

If, by pronouncing the A spiritually and physically, the student succeeds in calling forth this feeling of lightness internally and externally at will — even though he might not be thinking Kabbalistically of the feeling of lightness, the feeling nevertheless arises automatically — he may regard these exercises as complete and go on to the next letter, the umlaut Ä.

The exercises with Ä are the same as with A, but instead of the feeling of lightness the student must perceive and experience the opposite, namely a leaden heaviness. He must understand how to extend the feeling of heaviness to the whole universe and, vice versa, pass through this feeling of heaviness represented and effected by the letter Ä, from its expansion over the whole universe down to a very small point. When he has mastered the exercises with both A and Ä, the student may go on to the letter B.

B also has to do with the Earth element, with heaviness and gravity. The exercises have to be repeated until they are perfectly mastered.

I will now give the student the attributes of the elements which control the rest of the letters.

The C is subject to two elements: the Fire principle and the Air principle. Thus the student must sense and pass through two different feelings, a feeling of lightness combined with a feeling of warmth. This means that he learns to call forth the letter C with two elements, by causing, internally and externally, a sensation of warmth and lightness when pronouncing this letter.

D is controlled by the pure element of Fire; thus the Kabbalist must have a feeling of warmth alone when he utters it.

Depending on his concentration and his imaginative abilities, he must be able to increase this feeling to the level of heat.

The E has the specific attributes of the Akasha principle, which are revealed as a consequence of the effects of the elements through an all-penetrating feeling. The Kabbalist connects the exercises of the letter E with this all-penetrating feeling.

F pertains to the Earth principle and thus has the elemental attributes of heaviness and gravity. The exercises must therefore be combined with the feeling of heaviness and gravity.

G is subject to the principle of Water, so the exercises have to be combined with a feeling of coldness which must be increased to a feeling of iciness.

H pertains to the Fire principle, and the feeling vibrations are those of warmth.

The CH, as a letter of the Water principle, is to be practiced with the feeling of coldness.

I is a letter of the Earth element and must therefore be practiced with the feeling of heaviness and gravity.

The J — the Kabbalistic Jod — is attributed to the Fire principle in nearly all Kabbalistic writings. Only a few are aware that it is not the letter J that pertains to the Fire element, but the key word *Jod*, which represents the number 1, or omnipotence, in the Creation. In the Malkuth, 1 is a reflection of the key word of the number 10, by which the Kingdom of Earth is meant. The experienced Kabbalist will understand this analogy perfectly. Therefore, the letter J is not controlled by the Fire principle but by the Water principle, and must consequently be practiced with the vibrations of the feeling of coldness.

The K, with its Fire principle, is connected with the feeling of warmth and heat.

Like the letter A, the L is analogous to the Air element and requires the feeling-vibration of lightness.

M corresponds to the Prime Principle of Water and is to be practiced with a feeling of coldness. In the *Sepher Yetzirah* or *Book of Creation*, it is said that the Creator made the waters with the letter M.

The N, like the M, is subject to the Prime Principle of Water and must therefore also be connected with a feeling of coldness.

The O is a letter of the Earth element and must be practiced with a sensation of heaviness.

The work with umlaut Ö is most difficult. This umlaut has two seemingly contradictory elemental attributes, requiring the feeling of penetration and the feeling of heaviness and gravity. The vibration of the all-penetrating feeling expresses itself through the degree of density in the Akashic principle. The Akasha, as you know, corresponds to our Ether, which is the carrier of electrical and magnetic waves. Intuitive understanding in the Akasha is all-penetrating; it can also be condensed, and is expressed in its stability by umlaut Ö. In the beginning of this exercise, the Kabbalist will find it somewhat difficult to create the right harmony between these two opposing feelings. To make this practice easier, he should first practice the all-penetrating feeling in the belief that the Ö vibration expresses stability and density.

The same applies to the letter Ü, which may be regarded either as the letter Y or as the umlaut Ü, and which has the same elemental attributes, namely, the Etheric Earth principle and the all-penetrating feeling.

Next in line is P with the Earth principle, which is connected with the feeling of heaviness and gravity.[3]

---

[3]The letter R is missing in the first German edition. The original manuscript is no longer available–ED.

S and SCH are controlled by the Fire element, and consequently they have to be practiced with the feeling of warmth, one after the other. According to the *Sepher Yetzirah*, the active prime element of the Fire element was originally created by means of the letter SCH or Shin.

T, which also pertains to the Fire principle, is connected with a feeling of warmth.

The U is analogous to the pure Akasha principle and, when practiced, is connected with an all-penetrating feeling.

W, which comes under the fundamental principle of Water, is to be connected with a feeling of coldness.

Finally there is the letter Z, which is analogous to the Air principle and which must be practiced, in all phases, with a feeling of lightness.

Step IV
Kabbalisticae Elementorum

Only after having completely mastered the three preceding steps, in which the aspiring Kabbalist has learned to practice the letters one after another in accordance with the elements, may he commence the letters tripolarly in their alphabetical order. He initially begins his practice of each letter with two elements and then continues with three. The student must be able to imagine the letters in their colors and pronounce them with their phonetic pitches, i.e., their tones, and, at the same time, with the feeling connected with them as stipulated in the third step. If he achieves the ability to pronounce each letter in a tri-elemental way so as to cause the desired effect after extensive practice, he will be capable of using the letter Kabbalistically, i.e., creatively.

These exercises in the tri-elemental pronunciation of each letter will enable the student of Kabbalah to attain great magical abilities. For instance, he will become absolute master of the elements, achieve magical tenacity, and be able to resist any planetary vibration, even the densest ones. He will be invulnerable to any magical attack. His consciousness will expand so that he fully understands and recognizes the profundity of any term or any idea in the field of Hermetic science, not only intellectually but easily as regards the Akasha principle as well, in accordance with the universal laws. Not only does the Kabbalist thereby attain a higher magical knowledge, but, by his profound cognition, learns to reach the highest wisdom. Thus he develops not only into a knower but, what is much more, a true sage.

In the steps that follow, the student of the Kabbalah is taught to make practical use of each Kabbalistic letter with its fundamental ideas, in various planes as well as in the various spheres, first individually and later on in combinations, as words of power or words of creation. The person who studies the Kabbalah only theoretically will perhaps be able to understand, through intuition, the paragraphs that follow from a higher intellectual point of view — i.e., speaking Hermetically, from the philosophical point of view — though he will not be able to keep pace with the Kabbalistic practitioner in cognition and wisdom. Profound wisdom cannot be expressed by words, but only indicated by hints.

Thus the following exercises and the practical application of various Kabbalistic commands, and their uses as such, will only concern the practical Kabbalist; if a man of theory should attempt to apply the analogies indicated in the following chapter, they will remain ineffective for him.

Once more the Kabbalist will realize the extreme importance of the concentration exercises employing three senses, as detailed in my first book, *Initiation into Hermetics*. For in them he learned to call forth, at will, the expansiveness of an element within and outside of himself. One who has faultlessly mastered these concentration exercises of the three senses will have great success in the practical Kabbalah and will easily complete the tri-elemental exercises of the letters indicated here. But whoever has not undertaken the practical work of my course on the first Tarot card in my first book, and who now rushes into Kabbalah and Kabbalistic exercises without being properly prepared, will of course need much time for the completion of the exercises, since he must achieve the necessary abilities in concentration of the three senses.

In Step IV, the Kabbalist begins by practicing each letter, in sequence, tri-polarly (visually, acoustically and intuitively) in his whole body as though it were a hollow space, making them vibrate in their full resonance, condensing them and, finally, dissolving them again.

After having practiced the whole alphabet in his entire body, the exercises in the individual regions of his body will follow by pronouncing tri-elementally:

* the letters of the Fire element .... in the head
* the letters of the Air element .... in the chest
* the letters of the Water element ...... in the abdomen
* the letters of the Earth element .... in the legs and feet

It will be his next task to individually detach the regions of his microcosm in his consciousness.

1. The letters of the Fire element must be practiced inductively and deductively in the head in the following order:

First SCH and then S are pronounced phonetically as hissing sounds. Then follows the H, which must be perceived and practiced as a hot breath of air. Then comes letter D with the accompanying feeling of expansion, and finally the letters T and K with the feeling of a strong, explosive power.

As already remarked, the head must be imagined as an infinite hollow space in which the letter is pronounced a number of times in the mind, and then condensed to a small point in the appropriate color. The point, in its respective color, must be similar to a shining solar point. Each exercise must be accompanied by a feeling of enormous tension, a power of expansion. This power of tension and the imagined threefold concentrated form are to be retained as long as possible. The duration will depend on the student's ability to concentrate and will serve as a measure of his maturity. The exercise will be completed upon the dissolution of the sparkling letter point in the imaginal hollow space of the entire head. Also, during the procedure of dissolution, the concentration exercises of the three senses are to be adhered to until the end.

You may not begin with the next letter until you have perfectly mastered the one you are working with. After completing the exercises, the student must not feel or sense any unpleasant concomitant effects.

Anyone who tries to do the concentration exercises of the three senses without sufficiently preparing himself will become dizzy when simply attempting a mere immersion into the center of his head, and will experience headache, exhaustion, drowsiness, etc.

2. The letters analogous to the Air element follow and must be practiced in the chest by using the concentration exercises of the three senses. The inductive and deductive procedures must also be adhered to here.

The first letter A is practiced in the Air region as a long, drawn-out sound. After the A is mastered, Z comes next, pronounced with a hissing voice, and finally L, expressed as "laaaaaah."

The rest of the procedure is the same as has been described in regards to the head.

In the concentration exercises of the three senses, do not hold your breath. Breathing must remain uninfluenced by these exercises and any other concentration exercises; breathing must be regular.

If someone who is not prepared for this or who is not trained in concentration exercises involving the three senses should begin performing these exercises in the chest, he will immediately experience respiration problems and incur several injuries to his health, for instance pulmonary emphysema, asthma, and so on. Even various kinds of heart disease could ensue. A conscientious student, however, having gone through all the exercises in the proper sequence, will have nothing to fear; on the contrary, he will soon be convinced of the strengthening and harmonizing effects of the powers of each letter.

3. As soon as the student of the Kabbalah perfectly masters the Air region with its three letters both inductively and deductively, he can approach the region of the Water element, which is the abdominal region. He must imagine the entire abdominal region as being an infinite hollow space in which he will deal with the letters pertaining to the Water element in sequence, inductively as well as deductively.

The M is the first letter of the abdominal region, which must be practiced with a droning sound; the second letter is N, practiced with a humming sound. The third letter is W, to be pronounced softly; the fourth is J. Then follows the palatal sound CH in the fifth place and the palatal G in the sixth.

4. Finally, the student deals with the letters of the Earth element, which have to be practiced in the same manner in both legs, from the thighs to the tips of the toes. The letters of the Earth element are: I, O, F, R, B and P.

After having completed the exercises in the fourth region, the student must deal with C in the head and chest at the same time by imagining both regions, as a whole, to be an infinite hollow space in which the C is practiced, like the other letters, both inductively and deductively.

Then the student should transfer his consciousness into the center of his body, into the so-called medial section, the solar plexus, and imagine that his whole body is a hollow space in which he practices the letter U with his imagination and uses the concentration exercises of the three senses as an aid. Since the solar plexus is in the Akasha region, the student works neither inductively nor deductively, for he will know from my first book that the Akasha cannot be condensed. The letter U is the primal sound of the Akasha principle!

When this exercise is mastered, the letter E, which is also analogous to the Akasha principle, will be practiced. When exercising, a difference will make itself known in the vibration between the U and the E.

The last three remaining letters are to be practiced in the Earth region, namely umlaut Ö, umlaut Ü (Y) and umlaut Ä. These letters have an Akashic effect in the Earth region, and the practicing student will be able to differentiate the vibrations of these letters from each other and discover their specific Akashic attributes without effort; thus, for instance, that the Ä has a direct relation to the Ether of our material world, and so on.

The exercises indicated in this book serve the purpose of harmonizing the microcosm and the macrocosm by means of true Kabbalistic mysticism and preparing the microcosm for creative activities.

If the student now perfectly masters all the exercises hitherto indicated in this course, he will have come a great distance on the path of Kabbalistic mysticism. A microcosm or human being who is Kabbalistically prepared by these exercises not only resembles a creator on a small scale but, by virtue of the laws of analogy, is invisibly connected through his own microcosm, his miniature world, to all of the spheres of our planetary system. These exercises enable the student to achieve the perfect consciousness of the micro- and macrocosm, which in the Orient is often called the *Nirvakalpa Samadhi*. Unfortunately, most Europeans totally misinterpret this expression. Actually, *Nirvakalpa Samadhi* is, as already indicated, the micro- and macrocosmic consciousness, and thus a state of maturity of the highest Kabbalistic development which can only be attained after decades of practicing on the path of perfection. Usually, one incarnation is not sufficient for this. However, since time and space do not exist for an initiate on his way to perfect development, he may go on to attain in his next incarnation what he has not been able to achieve in a single lifetime of tireless work.

In the next steps, the Kabbalist will be taught how to use the different letters Kabbalistically.

Step V
The Ten Kabbalistic Keys

The preceding four steps of this course may be regarded, so to speak, as a preparation for the Kabbalistic or creative mode of action. The fifth step teaches the Kabbalist, in detail, the ten Kabbalistic keys, by which the numbers from 1 to 10 are to be understood and in which I will discuss their analogous relations. Of course, I cannot specify all the analogies of the numbers 1 to 10, since this subject alone would fill a voluminous book. Therefore I shall confine myself to giving some examples which will enable the intuitive student to discover further relations himself. The numbers 1-10 are Kabbalistic cardinal numbers corresponding to the divine primordial ideas with which the visible and the invisible world was created.

One

One is the first number in the universe and represents the highest form, the Deity Itself. The manifested light and everything that was made of it is God in His oneness, which is also reflected in all other numbers in all possible states of manifestation. Very wisely, the number 1 is called Kether, "the Crown," in the Hebrew Kabbalah. Whenever the Deity was to be identified, it was done by the number 1.

Some systems, especially the Kabbalistic system, also mention the zero, the so-called Ain Soph, but this is incomprehensible, unimaginable for man, and only serves as a hint that, apart from the number 1, nothing else and nothing higher can exist that would be comprehensible to the human spirit. Graphically speaking, 1 is symbolized by a dot which represents, in the different systems, the symbol of divine unification, of becoming one with God.

Anyone who, out of ignorance, begins his spiritual development immediately with the number 1 will sooner or later end with the number 10, for 1 represents omnipotence and 10 represents the deepest humility. The systems of initiation which begin with the number 1 are indiscriminately called monistic systems in Hermetic science. The Kabbalist should always be aware of the fact that the number 1 signifies the highest cognition, highest unity, highest wisdom. All primary ideas taken together form the One — God in His Revelation. According to the Bible, the number 1 is identified with the first day of creation, when God said "Let there be light!" (*Fiat Lux*)! Apart from many other things, all evolution begins with this number.

Two

Two is the number of duality, of polarity, of the positive and negative principles; thus, for instance, of good and evil, truth and falsehood. In the material sense, 2 indicates electricity and magnetism, love and hate, light and shadow. In short, it always represents a pole and its anti-pole, of which one could not exist without the other or be differentiated from the other. Kabbalistically seen, it refers to God and man. The number 2 pertains to those religious systems which regard the Deity as something separate, whether in regards to form, shape, a specific attribute or prime idea whereby the dualistic principle is to be found in all forms of existence. 2 also indicates an attitude towards the micro- and macrocosm, of whatever kind. Graphically, the number 2 is represented by a horizontal line.

Three

This number is graphically symbolized by a triangle. 3 is the number of the Akasha principle, of fate, of karma, and, in terms of planetary correspondences, of the sphere of Saturn. Everything past, present and future, the mental as well as the astral and the material, originates from the Akasha principle, wherein the 3 is also to be found. 3 is the original idea of procreation, which expresses itself in the plus and minus, in the man and woman who, in unification, procreate the third, the child. In man himself, the 3 is represented by spirit, soul and body. 3 is also the number of intuition. According to destiny, all religious systems are derived from this number. 3 is the number of life and death. It is the number of complete cognition in its highest form.

Four

This number is the highest number for the experienced Kabbalist as far as his practice is concerned, for it is a perfect representation of the Tetragrammatonic Principle. In the planetary system, the number 4 is attributed to Jupiter. This number represents all four basic elements: Fire, Air, Water and Earth; the four points of the compass: east, west, south and north; the four fundamental attributes of God: omnipotence, wisdom, love and immortality — full consciousness. 4, therefore, is the number by which everything was created and realized in the micro- and the macrocosm; it is the number of law, order, justice and realization. At the same time, 4 is the number of everything that was created in the visible and the invisible worlds. As a divine prime idea, 4 signifies the highest wisdom. It is the number of plus and minus in the aspect of effect. It is also the number of length, width, height and depth. Graphically or symbolically, the number 4 is represented by a cross whose arms are of equal length, or by an equilateral square.

Five

This number is the perfect representation of the microcosm, that is, of man in all his phases and forms of existence. In the number 5 the activities of the four elements in human beings are reflected, and are directed by the fifth element, the Akasha. The intuitive Kabbalist will recognize that not only does the number 5 symbolize the elements dominating man, but so does its Kabbalistic numerical order; for 5 is half of 10, and 10 stands for the whole creation. The microcosm or miniature world, human-kind, must be represented in its completeness by half of 10. Since the working of the four elements, dominated by the Akasha, is represented by the number 5, this number also represents strength and power, pertaining to the planet Mars. Consequently, everything that expresses an active power or might is in harmony with the number 5. All influences that are effected by the power and might of a human being belong to this number. All active magic belongs to this sequence of numbers. The number 5 is graphically represented by an equilateral pentagram, also called a pentagon.

Six

In contrast to 5, which represents the microcosm, man in his perfection, the number 6 represents the macrocosm in its perfec-tion. Graphically, the number 6 is expressed by an equilateral hexagram. Seen from the Kabbalistic point of view, the two interlacing triangles point to the manifested light, to life and also to the possible bond with God. The hexagram is also the symbol of the magician who, after having struggled through to the sixth sphere, the sphere of the Sun, may attain a bond with God. This means that the Kabbalist must rise spiritually and astrally to the Kabbalistic 6, the solar sphere, if he wants to achieve a connec-tion to the number 1, to God. 6 is the visible symbol of the *Emerald Tablet of Hermes,* which begins with the words: "That which is above is like that which is below." The lower triangle of the hexagram denotes, in the magical sense, man in his three-dimensional aspect of body, soul and spirit. The upper triangle of the hexagram points to the three-dimensional unification and influence of divine power, divine virtues, etc., mentally, astrally and physically, in their connection from above to below.

As already mentioned, the number 6 represents the Sun, called Tiphareth in the Kabbalah. From the physical point of view, it is our own sun, around which the planets revolve. Apart from this, macrocosmic magic, the magic of the spheres, is also expressed by the number 6. Many more analogies to the number 6 could be indicated, but the examples given above will be sufficient for the Kabbalist.

Seven

Seven is the number of harmony, fertility, fecundation and growth. It is also the number of love in all its phases, whether one is dealing with the lowest form of love or with its highest cosmic aspect. Mercy, benevolence, virtue and happiness are also aspects of love and therefore pertain to the number 7. Furthermore, 7 is the number of beauty, purity and equilibration. With regard to astrology, 7 is the number of Venus, so that all methods and practices of Venus magic or scale magic also belong to this numerical category. Among other things, the seven basic notes of the musical octave are also analogous to the number 7, and so are the seven tattwas, the seven states of maturity of the spirit (chakras), etc. The graphic representation of the number 7 is an equilateral heptagon (septangle). There are, however, other symbols for the number 7; for instance, a large triangle with a square in its center or, vice versa, a square with a triangle in its center, depending on the number to be entered graphically. The square is sometimes replaced by a cross with arms of equal length which is drawn in the center of a triangle. By doing this, one gets seven points, thus alluding to the number 7. There are many other analogies to this number, for example the seven colors of the spectrum, the colors of the rainbow, etc. It will be the student's task to discover most of the analogies for himself.

Eight

This is the number of the mind, the intellect, and thus the number of knowledge. Everything that comes under the scope of the intellect pertains to the number 8. It is also the number of the spirit, of the mental body. In astrology, 8 is analogous to Mercury. Its symbolic expression is the octagon, formed by two interlacing squares. One square symbolizes the lawfulness of the activities of the four elements, while the other square represents man in his tetrapolar aspect, the tetrapolar magnet equipped with the four fundamental attributes of the spirit: will, intellect, feeling and consciousness, without which there is no knowledge. The octagon is simultaneously a symbol of the positive and the negative effects of the elements in the micro- and macrocosm. It stands to reason that all theoretical knowledge, besides any knowledge of magic, Kabbalah or any other science of this type, belongs to this number.

Nine

Through the nonagon, three interlacing equilateral triangles graphically represent the number 9. It symbolizes the prime idea of the astral world, the astral body, and everything else belonging to the astral, including all its analogies, characteristics, etc. At the same time, 9 is the number of motion, of rhythm, and thus of life in its most subtle form. Under its aspects come all practices of astral magic, of the magic of nature and mumia. 9 is the number which prepares every situation in the astral world for the material world. 9 is analogous to the Moon, and everything coming under the lunar sphere and its influence is represented by it. 9 is, of course, the highest number, too; any number can be reduced to the units 1 to 9 by the sum of their digits. Although the number 9 has many other analogies, these few indications will have to do for the student of the Kabbalah.

Ten

In the order of the ten Kabbalistic keys, which correspond to the numbers 1-10, the number 10 is the last. It is the reflection of the number 1 in its coarsest form. 10 is the number of physical matter, the number of realization, of cohesion, and of the Earth element with all its aspects. Not without good reason is the number 10 called "the Kingdom" (Malkuth) in the Hebrew Kabbalah. 10 is the number by which everything that has been physically created (matter in its densest form) in both the microcosm and the macrocosm is to be understood. The entire human body in its material form is subject to the number 10. By the same logic, so is the mineral kingdom with all its degrees of density, its substances, ores, etc.; furthermore, so are the vegetable kingdom and the animal kingdom; in short, everything that we can perceive with our material senses. The number 10 points to the beginning of physical matter. It is the starting point on the path to God. All the influences of the prime ideas described earlier in this book, beginning with the incarnated Deity on our earth and proceeding downward to the lowest materialization or condensation, are expressed by the number 10.

The number 10 is graphically represented by the alchemical symbol of a circle with a cross consisting of eight arms in its center, contrary to number 1, which is usually symbolized by a dot or a circle as the sign of infinity. However, the number 10 may also be expressed symbolically by a square with a circle drawn in its center.

Each science, including Hermetics, proceeds from the number 10. From a Kabbalistic point of view, 10 is the number not only of the material world but of the zone girdling the earth. These few correspondences must be sufficient to enable the Kabbalist to discover further analogies himself.

★

The ten Sephiroth which are mentioned in every Kabbalistic book and which also have reference to the numbers 1 to 10, are attributed to the divine prime ideas. The experienced Kabbalist will see that all religious systems, all magical working systems, and all Kabbalistic keys may be reduced to the numbers 1-10.

To count Kabbalistically means to understand and master all these keys perfectly, all these numbers and their analogies. The greatness of this science of the Kabbalistic numbers from 1 to 10, and the profound wisdom contained therein, will be clear from what has already been said.

When the Creator fashioned His perfect image, man, He bestowed upon him the shape in which the ten fundamental ideas become visible, the ten fingers on his hands and the ten toes on his feet, which are evidence of his perfection. The Kabbalah therefore justly regards the numbers from 1 to 10 as the most perfect of numbers. It has already been said in one of the preceding chapters that the five fingers on man's right hand and the five on his left have a certain relationship to the prime ideas of the ten Sephiroth. The five fingers on his right hand have reference to the numbers 1 through 5, and the five fingers on his left hand to the numbers 6 through 10. The hands with their ten fingers are therefore analogous to the prime ideas expressed by the numbers from 1 to 9, while the ten toes alone refer to the number 10, in which the lowest plane, the earth, is expressed symbolically.

There are Kabbalistic gestures with the fingers held in certain positions, accompanied by Kabbalistic words of power (commands) in analogy to the ten prime ideas, with which one may work magically. From what has been said, an experienced Kabbalist will be able to compose his own working methods for magico-Kabbalistic practices by using finger positions.

These brief hints will be sufficient for him. If anyone should be especially interested in the magic of Kabbalistic gestures, he will of course be able to obtain detailed methods from the spiritual beings who know about it; this is merely to draw his attention to the possibilities.

Step VI
The Tetragrammaton
Jod-He-Vau-He
The Tetrapolar Kabbalistic Key

After adequate completion of the first five steps of this course, the Kabbalist will certainly reach the conclusion that it is important to master the indicated numerical analogies well if he wants to comprehend, through numbers, not only all ideas, but also everything that seems desirable to him and which is determined in accordance with numbers; for due to analogous connections the lawfulness of an idea is expressed by number. From a Kabbalistic point of view, numbers are laws! The Kabbalist must be capable, through the number combinations 1-10, of arriving at the corresponding prime ideas, a practice which, in the Hebrew Kabbalah, is called Gematria. The individual numbers 1-10 represent all prime ideas in their purest and highest form. Two-digit numbers stand for everything astral. Numbers with three or more digits refer to the material world with its lawful effects. When composing Kabbalistic words of power, formulas, etc., this knowledge is of utmost importance, for words expressed by numbers represent lawfulness and the powers connected with it.

The Kabbalist will learn more about this lawfulness when applying certain letters and letter combinations to serve particular purposes and to bring about particular effects.

As soon as the Kabbalist, after diligent studies, has learned to count Kabbalistically from 1 to 10 and thus to classify, in a Kabbalistic sense, each thing, idea, or cause and effect with regard to its respective prime idea, he will have achieved a great deal. And unless the Kabbalist has attained this ability, he should not proceed. By diligent comparisons and analogous conclusions, he will learn to reduce combinations of letters to their prime ideas and to fully understand their effects and lawfulness. In doing this, his intuition will serve him well. By speculative procedures and mere knowledge — i.e., with the intellect alone — he will hardly be successful in fully grasping the lawfulness of the numbers from 1 to 10 with all their analogies.

In the passages that follow, we shall reflect on the alphabet, in its sequence, from the Kabbalistic point of view. The Kabbalistic knowledge of the letters and their analogies will depend on the understanding of the Kabbalistic keys, the numbers from 1 to 10 as indicated earlier. The reader and Kabbalist will find it understandable that for technical reasons I am unable to deal with all the analogies of each letter, and must confine myself to a small number of analogies which occur frequently in practice. If the Kabbalist should succeed in learning the analogies of all the letters, it will then be possible for him to be creatively active with all these letters, with the help of the concentration exercises of the three senses.

The application of the first key serves the purpose of pronouncing letters Kabbalistically out of the Akasha principle so that they are realized either on the mental, astral or material plane. When the Kabbalist transfers his consciousness into the Akasha principle and, with the help of concentration exercises of the three senses, utters a letter combined with the wish that a timeless and spaceless cause be created, the effect analogous to this letter will be released in the mental world — the spirit or mental body — where neither time nor space exist.

If, on the other hand, the Kabbalist pronounces a letter in the Akasha principle while giving it a certain shape, the cause created in analogy to this letter will take that shape and the analogous effect will be released on the astral plane, the astral body of the human being, since the astral plane and astral body are bound to space, to form.

Should the effects relate not only to the astral world but also, through the Kabbalist's wish, to the material plane, the created causes will lead to situations in the astral world which will then release material effects. Through this the Kabbalist will see that shapes are analogous to situations in the astral world and that effects on the material plane can be called forth from the astral world.

Now, if the Kabbalist pronounces a letter Kabbalistically in the Akasha principle and thereby creates causes which he limits to time and space, thus giving them temporal and spatial limitation, these causes will have their effects analogous to the Akasha principle on the material plane, passing directly over the mental and astral worlds. This occurs without having to form relevant situations in the astral world for the purpose of their realization.

Reiterated in a few words, it is possible for the Kabbalist to directly influence, by just one letter, the mental, astral or material plane from the highest authority, the Akasha principle. This influence is always effected by just one letter. From the Kabbalistic point of view, such letters are called single letters.

Many books claim that the first ten letters correspond to the divine prime ideas. However, it is not the ten letters that are the key but the use of the whole alphabet, although in each case the Akasha principle is stimulated by just a single letter and from there the realization is effected in accordance with the respective wish concentration. Therefore, when creating causes by means of a single letter, the space and time relationship is the first key with which the Kabbalist can work creatively in all three planes of the small and great world, the micro- and macrocosm, and in all planetary spheres.

Only when the Kabbalist can work faultlessly with this first key may he proceed to the practical application of the second key. In his work with the second key the Kabbalist will not start from the Akasha principle, but directly from the mental kingdom; and he will first work Kabbalistically in the mental plane, then in the astral plane, and finally in the material world as well.

The second Kabbalistic key requires the use of two letters at the same time, which will then call forth the desired cause and release the effect. In the mental world, time and space are not transferred into the cause. In the astral world, the cause is likewise created by two letters, but there the shape and form of expression is also given when the letters are spoken Kabbalistically, in order to cause direct effects on the astral world or the astral body. If, however, a realization in the material world is intended, then the situations necessary for such a realization are created directly in the astral world by the elements, which then release the desired effect on the material plane. When, in the Kabbalistic application of two letters analogous to the planned effects, the letters are transferred into their causes in the mental world, at the same time being given a certain form of expression and a termination in time, the realization will take place in the mental world and the effect will become evident in the material world after directly passing through the astral world, without having caused the necessary situation in the astral world. It stands to reason that direct Kabbalistic effects can be caused in this manner in all three kingdoms of the material world as well, namely the mineral, vegetable and animal kingdoms.

If the Kabbalist also masters the second Kabbalistic key perfectly, he may try the third key. When applying this key, causes in the astral world will be created which will then have their effects on the mental as well as the astral and material worlds. With this key, three letters are Kabbalistically applied. It should be understood that the term "Kabbalistically applied" refers to the pronunciation of letters while using the concentration exercises of three senses.

When working with three letters, the same procedure is to be followed as with the application of only two letters. If the

Kabbalist utters three letters in the astral world without any indication of time or space, the cause will be created in the astral world; it will, however, have no effect on the astral or material world, but only, and directly, on the mental plane.

If, in the use of three letters, the spatial relationships are also considered in Kabbalistic utterance, there will be no effect on the mental world, and cause and effect will develop only in the astral sphere or astral plane, or, if desired, in the astral body. If three letters are transferred Kabbalistically into the astral world, taking into consideration that the spatial relations and the analogous effects of the created causes are not of an astral but of a material nature, then their realization in the material world is brought about by the elements and their fluids.

If three letters are transferred Kabbalistically into the astral world and, in so doing, temporal and spatial relationships are taken into consideration, then the influence will be exerted directly from the astral world upon the material plane without the necessity of creating the situations otherwise required for realization.

The use of the third Kabbalistic key may be repeated in a few words: using this key means working Kabbalistically with three letters, with effects on the mental world without temporal and spatial relations, with effects on the astral plane with spatial relationships or circumstances, and finally with effects on the material world with spatial and temporal relationships simultaneously.

The Kabbalist will be unable to make use of the fourth and last key described herein until he has mastered the third Kabbalistic key perfectly.

In the last, the so-called tetrapolar key, one works with four letters with which one can be effective directly from the material world. The same procedure is adhered to in this case as with the other keys, whether affecting the mental world from the material world, working without the conception of space and time, or causing effects on the astral plane using the conception of spatial circumstances, or affecting the material world directly, simultaneously using the concepts of time and space.

Thus I have described the practical use of the tetrapolar key, the mystery of the Tetragrammaton, the so-called Jod-He-Vau-He, as seen from the Kabbalistic point of view in consideration of its application. The four-lettered name of God is herewith exhausted as regards its practical use. The Kabbalist who has honestly struggled with himself up to this point will now actually be able to work creatively by using the four-letter key — the Tetragrammatonic key — in all spheres, all planes, in the microcosm and the macrocosm. From the Kabbalistic point of view, he will have attained the same power that was applied by the Creator Himself in His act of creation, when creating the world in all three kingdoms.

Having arrived at this level of development, a Kabbalist is usually chosen by Divine Providence as a servant, and given a suitable mission to undertake. The best service becomes evident by the highest devotion to and profoundest humility towards Divine Providence that a human being is capable of feeling. Whoever has achieved this degree of maturity will never abuse his power and creative abilities.

This tetrapolar key is the lost word, the key to the name of God that has been lost; it is the genuine and correct pronunciation of the divine name, and, as justly claimed by the Kabbalists, this key is the mystery of creation, it is God in His revelation.

There exist six more keys, which, however, are not for Kabbalistic application on our earth or in the zone girdling the earth, but which only serve the spheric Kabbalah. I have not been allowed by Divine Providence to give any details on these keys. However, the Kabbalist who masters the tetrapolar key, the Tetragrammatonic key or true Jod-He-Vau-He, and who is able to apply it practically, will also be trusted with the other keys by Divine Providence, especially when the Kabbalist is designated for certain missions that have to be carried out in those spheres that lie outside the zone girdling the earth.

To obtain a better overview, I will reiterate once more that the single key is the simplest key, the key that you will most easily be able to make your own. When applying it, the Kabbalist need only pronounce a letter Kabbalistically in his spirit, with the consciousness of his spirit. In the case of the two-letter and three-letter keys, the letters have to be pronounced with the consciousness of the spirit and the astral body. When the tetrapolar key is used, the letters have to be pronounced Kabbalistically with the consciousness, with the perspective of the spirit, and with the astral and material bodies. The Kabbalist must thus be conscious of these three forms of existence in his body.

In this step I have entrusted the Kabbalist with the greatest Kabbalistic mystery, namely the practical use of the tetrapolar key, the key of realization by the Word. For thousands of years this mystery has been strictly guarded. With the permission of Divine Providence, this secret of how God created the earth and how He works creatively may now be entrusted to mature human beings. Whoever deals with this book more than theoretically will fully understand the extent of the sphere of influence.

Step VII
The Kabbalistic Mysticism
Of the Alphabet
The First Key
The One-Letter Key

In this step I shall indicate some of the analogies of the letters which are most important for Kabbalistic and magical purposes. If I attempted to describe all the analogies of letters that have reference to the mental and astral kingdoms and to the material world, I should at the same time have to give an account of the whole world in all its forms of existence; but of course this would be impossible. However, with the keys he has already been given, the Kabbalist has reached a point where he is able to compose further analogies himself, on the basis of logical conclusions and depending upon the powers he wants to contact or work with. The advanced Kabbalist also knows that the letters may be related to everything that has been created. The following details may therefore serve him as further guiding principles for his studies of the Kabbalah and allow him to penetrate even deeper into the correlations.

A description of all the letters of our alphabet follows.

A

Akasha: In the Akasha principle, the A symbolizes the highest wisdom and the highest illumination that can ever be bestowed upon a human being. At the same time, it represents the purity of all ideas in all forms of existence.

Mental: In the mental plane of man, the A represents, as a fundamental attribute, the enlightened intellect. All the parallels which must be brought into harmony with the enlightened

119

intellect — such as discernment, understanding, cognition of the most profound truths, high knowledge and perception, the awakening of all intellectual abilities, etc. — are expressed in the mental world by the A and through its vibration.

Astral: All talents, attributes and abilities that are subject to the Air principle — e.g., musical talent, eloquence, poetic ability, and so on — may be called forth in the astral kingdom by the use of the letter A. In respect to the occult abilities there are, besides others, clairvoyance, clairaudience, the art of levitation, the control over the Air element and its beings (meaning in the kingdom of the element itself as well as in the astral kingdom), and the control of all powers analogous to the Air principle which occur in the astral world. The language of symbols, especially their understanding and power, may also be attained by the letter A.

Matter: In the material world, the control of the Air principle and all its analogies may be achieved by the letter A, whether expressed as control of the Air spirits, control of storms, or whatever. By Kabbalistic utterance of the letter A, a doctor or naturopath may successfully treat any illness of the chest.

Practice: The practical application of the letter A begins from the Akasha principle; that is, the Kabbalist first visualizes his material body, then his astral body (which has the same shape as his material body), then the spirit dwelling in the astral body, the "I." At the same time, he meditates on the connection between his material body and the physical world, his astral body and the astral world, and his mental body and the mental world. In his meditations, he continues with the consciousness that he is not only pronouncing the letter A with his physical voice, but with his spirit, soul and body simultaneously. Then he meditates on the attributes and analogies of the A as indicated, by intuitively comprehending the prime ideas with his consciousness in the Akasha principle. And further: parallel to the Akasha principle, the mental world manifests itself in the intellect and from there is realized in the astral and eventually in the material world.

After these meditations, the Kabbalist transfers himself, with his consciousness, into the Akasha principle by sensing that he is a point in his solar plexus, his own microcosm, calling forth a spaceless and timeless state, a state of trance.

The practice of transferring oneself into the Akasha principle to induce a state of trance has been described in my first book, *Initiation into Hermetics.*

As soon as the Kabbalist feels himself to be the center, the focal point of his microcosm, and senses his whole body as an infinite space, he utters the letter A in the three-dimensional way into the whole universe. The universe is filled, in the microcosm, with the relevant color; with the letter A it is a light blue color, along with the note G-major and the consciousness of all-penetrating wisdom and enlightenment.

Doing this, the Kabbalist may repeat the A a few times in his spirit. In these exercises, however, a great emphasis need not be placed on the color and the tone, for the Kabbalist has already taken the analogies into consideration by his concentration exercises of the three senses; however, the greatest care must be devoted to the virtues and attributes and the analogous ideas. On concluding this exercise, the Kabbalist must return his consciousness to its normal state, and thereafter meditate on the relationships of the A in more detail.

The Kabbalist who repeats these exercises will realize that, depending on his maturity, diligence and perseverance, the virtues analogous to each letter will somehow be expressed in his mental and spiritual as well as in his astral and material bodies, in a mental, astral and material manner.

Only when perfectly mastering one letter — which requires a longer period of practice — should the Kabbalist go on to the next exercises. It is useless to perform exercises with subsequent letters until the preceding letter is completely mastered and unless the Kabbalist is able to call forth, at will, any letter in the Akasha principle. Persistent exercises will teach the Kabbalist to perceive the connections, vibrations, powers and spheres of influence more and more clearly, and he will later be able to apply each letter from other planes, too. The more perseverance he can muster with these exercises — without hurrying — the better his progress will be.

I remember having students who had to practice the one-letter key in the manner described for as long as half a year, but were very successful later on. The old adage "Haste makes waste" is especially applicable in the beginning of these exercises, before the Kabbalist has learned to transfer his consciousness into all regions and to speak there in a Kabbalistic, three-dimensional manner; and, furthermore, before he grasps and learns to understand the analogous ideas, abilities and powers, and to properly grasp and experience the contrary relationships.

The mastery of each subsequent letter will then be so much easier. One who is proficient in the Kabbalah is able to make use, in a few moments, not only of one letter but of whole formulas, whether from the Akasha principle or a subordinate plane, just as he pleases. In the beginning, difficulties will arise with regard to the imagination or conscious sentience of the analogous virtues, powers, might, and so on, of the respective letter in the Akasha principle. Frequent repetition of the exercises will enable the Kabbalist to envision the relevant virtues and to perceive them consciously. Later on, when he has sufficiently expanded his consciousness, it will be easy for him to consciously accept any abstract idea, no matter how profound and penetrating it may be; in short, he will be able to digest it spiritually.

It has already been mentioned, earlier in this book, that the letter A is subject to the Air element and is controlled by the electrical fluid, influencing the chest and lungs in the material world.

B

B is to be practiced in the same way as the letter A; the individual steps are also the same. I shall now describe all the other letters, one after the other, mentioning some of their analogies in the Akasha principle, the mental, astral and material worlds. Before each exercise, the Kabbalist must visualize in his consciousness all the analogies and must be able to pronounce the respective letter Kabbalistically in the Akasha principle, in a spaceless and timeless state, and to connect it with its respective powers, virtues, etc.

Akasha: In the Akasha principle, the letter B indicates the perception of universal life; furthermore, it indicates the cognition of polarity in all forms of existence, which will lead to the most profound wisdom. With the letter B the Kabbalist will learn to comprehend fully the plus and the minus; it will become quite clear to him that nothing has been created in vain and that the negative as well as the positive must exist, for without these opposites one could not be differentiated from the other.

Mental: The mastery of the letter B will give the Kabbalist complete power over the electric and magnetic fluids in all the spheres and planes. The Kabbalist will thereby become master over life and death and attain the power to change any fate. But he will never cause a change in the established karma of any human being without good reason and the approval of Divine Providence, nor will he cause any chaos.

Astral: The mastery of the letter B in his astral body will impart to the Kabbalist the ability to call forth magico-Kabbalistic volts, to charge Kabbalistic talismans and bring about sexual-magical effects. Everything that is connected to polarity in the astral kingdom will become completely clear to the Kabbalist. He will become acquainted with the most profound mysteries and attain a faculty of intuition that cannot be described in words.

Matter: B represents all the laws of polarization on our earth and gives expression to them in matter. The Kabbalist thereby becomes complete master over the electric and magnetic fluids in the physical world. Apart from that, by mastering the letter B he is given the might to remedy any disharmony in the human body — that is, to cure any disease — and to charge analogous remedies Kabbalistically. Furthermore, he obtains the might of controlling life and death in the three kingdoms of the material world as well.

From the examples given here, the Kabbalist may see in what way and for what purposes a letter is to be applied Kabbalistically, and what abilities can be procured with just one letter. In the course of time, and by continuous exercises, the Kabbalist will extend his knowledge and increase his practical experience.

When the Kabbalist has achieved everything which pertains to the letter B, which is only possible after long practice, he may proceed to deal with the next letter Kabbalistically.

C

Akasha: In the Akasha principle, the letter C embodies all the mysteries of the Eucharist in all its aspects. The C vibration symbolizes the mystery of self-spiritualization and, at the same time, the great mystery of transformation. He who masters this mystery well shall comprehend and recognize the profundity of the Eucharist and its aspects and will master all the practical methods relating to the Eucharist. From the Hermetic point of view, the practices mentioned in my first book, *Initiation into Hermetics,* in the chapter dealing with the magic of water, belong to the practical application of the Eucharist in its lowest sense. In the Kabbalistic use of the letter C, however, the point in question is a higher aspect of the Eucharist, for it has to do with the transformation or incorporation of a divine idea, a higher virtue, into a certain form.

Mental: All practices dealing with the question of influencing one's own mental body, or someone else's spirit, by way of a divine idea, virtue, attribute, power, might, etc., fall into the category and vibration of the letter C.

Astral: In the astral body and the astral plane, the Kabbalist learns to know the profound mystery of the Eucharist — that is, the astral impregnation with one of the said virtues, qualities, and so on, by the vibration of the letter C. However, the vibration of the C not only influences the impregnation of the astral body but also the mummification of the same and the control of the astral aura.

Matter: Through the C vibration, the Kabbalist learns to stimulate the entire matter and to equip it with mental as well as astral virtues, powers, etc. By this letter, he also learns to Kabbalistically impregnate any material form at will. Furthermore, the true Kabbalistic alchemy is also influenced by this letter vibration. By the term "Kabbalistic alchemy," the changing of matter by way of the Word is to be understood, which is equivalent to endowing it with another quality.

D

Akasha: In the Akasha principle, the letter D influences all the mysteries of creation through its vibration, namely the mysteries of the act of creation in the micro- and macrocosm respectively. Not only are the laws of creation expressed by this letter, but, when mastering the D vibration, all cognition is revealed to the Kabbalist. Since the macro- and the microcosms are subject to the same laws, the Kabbalist learns to know and master the micro- as well as the macrocosm from the standpoint of the profoundest wisdom with regard to the creation and all its analogies.

Mental: With this letter vibration, the Kabbalist learns to know and completely control, with the entire "I" consciousness, his own mental matrix as well as those of other people in the mental plane, or rather, in the mental body. The profoundest wisdom of the spirit in every phase (elemental analogies), and the profoundest cognition with regard to the "I" consciousness, will be bestowed upon the Kabbalist by the vibration of the letter D.

Astral: All erotic aspects that are analogous to the astral body will be revealed to the Kabbalist with the D vibration. All the methods of love magic and sex magic in every aspect of the four elements become accessible to him, practically as well as theoretically, with this letter vibration, so that he becomes a perfect master of love in all its phases and aspects.

Matter: In the material world, the vibration of the letter D controls everything relating to fecundation. The practical application of this vibration in the material world is so manifold that it would fill an entire book. This, of course, is impossible for technical reasons. For example: a seed may be fertilized by mastery of the vibration of the letter D; furthermore, the shape of a future entity may already be recognized from a portion of semen; a grain of seed may be ennobled; the male semen may be impregnated with the virtues, qualities, etc., that the future child will have; the future fate of a fruit growing from any seed may not only be judged but influenced. All progenitive acts — everything that is given life by procreation — fall under this letter vibration.

E

Akasha: In the Akasha principle, this letter vibration represents the omni-consciousness which also represents, as a divine idea and virtue, its omnipresence in everything that has ever been created. This letter vibration will unite the Kabbalist's normal consciousness with the omni-consciousness or cosmic consciousness, so that the Kabbalist who calls forth this letter vibration in the Akasha principle is, at the same time, omnipresent himself. In Hermetic science, this connection with the omni-consciousness (or with the omnipresence) is called cosmic consciousness, and in the corresponding Oriental traditions it is called *Nirvakalpa Samadhi*.

Mental: In the mental kingdom, in the mental body or the spirit, this letter vibration will call forth the highest form of intuition. It confers upon the Kabbalist the mental attribute of the universal transference of his consciousness. In this state there is no perception of time and space. Divinity in Its highest form speaks through this letter vibration.

Astral: In the astral body, the vibration of the letter E represents control of the astral consciousness, whether of oneself or of others. Specifically, the ability of exceptional clairaudience can easily be achieved through this letter vibration. By the ability of exceptional clairaudience, not only do we mean the ability to hear the voices of other entities, etc., but also the understanding of the language of all animals and the acoustical perception of the remotest past, present, and even future, regardless of any distance or kingdom, i.e., the human or animal kingdom.

Matter: By mastering this letter vibration, the profoundest mysteries of materialization to condensation and demateriallization to refinement are unfolded to the Kabbalist. The Kabbalist will learn to condense any idea or concept, any mental or astral form in such a way as to render it physically visible. The condensation of this letter vibration gave existence to everything material — to physical matter and also to the mysteries of the opposite procedure by which everything material may be transferred back into its refined and most subtle form. All the mysteries relating to materialization and dematerialization will become quite clear to the Kabbalist who uses this letter. At the same time, he attains the ability to apply all this knowledge in practice.

F

Akasha: In the Akasha principle, the letter F represents the lawfulness and harmony of all visible worlds, the micro- and macrocosm. By using this letter, the Kabbalist will learn to recognize lawfulness as the most perfect harmony, and furthermore to observe the operation and the laws of analogy of the macro- and microcosms in their truest form. One who perfectly masters this letter in the Kabbalistic sense will be able to determine at once the analogous lawfulness of any idea.

Mental: In the mental kingdom, this letter vibration represents the unification and the dependency of the four fundamental attributes of the spirit; namely: the will, intellect, feeling (life), and consciousness in its entirety. With the vibration of the letter F, the Kabbalist learns to understand the lawfulness, in the mental kingdom, of these four fundamental attributes, as well as their analogous correlations. At the same time, he is able to control, at will, these fundamental attributes of the spirit, within himself and others. This clearly shows that the Kabbalist thereby becomes the perfect master of his own spirit as well as the spirit of any other human being.

Astral: The mastery of this letter vibration allows the Kabbalist to recognize and control the mysteries of the tetrapolar magnet and the sphere of influence of the four elements in the astral kingdom. The Kabbalist acquires the ability to master any character trait, any virtue, with its respective element. Also, the mystery of magical equilibrium will become entirely clear to him, and he will be able to comprehend all the universal laws, all abstract ideas in their purest state.

Matter: In the material world, the mystery of the magic quadrature of the circle, the tetrapolar magnet, is revealed to the Kabbalist by the vibration of this letter. The Kabbalist not only learns to recognize this in its relation to the human body but to apply it, whether he wishes to bring this mystery into relationship with intellectual knowledge, physics, or metaphysics. The Kabbalist also acquires the ability to understand and apply in

128

practice the mystery of the Tetragrammaton, the Jod-He-Vau-He, with all methods and systems that require the use of the tetrapolar magnet.

G

Akasha: This letter vibration allows the Kabbalist to recognize, in the Akasha principle of all spheres and planes, the profundity of divine grace and mercy in all their aspects. It gives him the possibility to see how far divine lawfulness extends and how divine grace and mercy affect man and animal.

Mental: The virtue of divine peace in the spirit, the experience of peacefulness, is attainable through this letter vibration, and so is the blessing by Divine Providence in all its aspects. If the Kabbalist masters this letter vibration, he acquires the ability to bestow true divine blessing.

Astral: In the astral body and astral kingdom, the feeling of blissfulness, of complete satisfaction, may be obtained through this letter vibration. Likewise, when mastering this letter vibration, situations causing happiness, success and wealth in the material world may be Kabbalistically created by means of the elements and the electromagnetic fluid.

Matter: In the material world, this letter vibration represents all phases of prosperity and wealth, of happiness and contentment. Divine Providence has created abundance through this letter vibration, and, like the Creator, the Kabbalist may also bring about abundance in everything for himself or others should he wish to do so.

H

Akasha: In the Akasha principle, this letter represents the might of the Word. The Kabbalistic application of this letter in the Akasha principle allows the Kabbalist to understand and use the cosmic language Kabbalistically. The higher significance of such a possibility has already been pointed out in the theoretical part of this book. The mastery of the H vibration in the Akasha principle enables the Kabbalist to bestow to each letter dynamic, i.e., creative power. It is certain that by so doing he will become capable of couching any idea in Kabbalistic words.

Mental: In the mental kingdom, this letter vibration allows the Kabbalist to attain the ability to understand the activities of Divine Providence, and not only to perceive it with his intellect but to receive it symbolically, in the form of pictures, through his spiritual sight. By frequent repetition of the exercises with this letter vibration, the purest clairvoyance will also be achieved at the same time.

Astral: The mastery of the H vibration enables the Kabbalist to attain the ability to influence anyone's destiny at his discretion, and furthermore to fully comprehend, understand and apply all Kabbalistic systems, all mantric and Tantric practices in their truest forms. Whoever is able to call forth this letter vibration in the astral body as well — which requires great effort — may confidently expect to become a perfect Kabbalist.

Matter: With this letter vibration, the Kabbalist will learn to fully understand the practical use of the Kabbalah, the cosmic language, in all the kingdoms and forms of existence of the material world, and, apart from that, he will also gain the ability to work with it creatively. He learns to understand the full meaning of the words "Let it be," as indicated in the Kabbalah. That the ability to become a perfect master of the material world may thereby be attained is also quite evident.

CH

Akasha: In the Akasha principle, the virtues of clarity and perfect purity are manifested by the vibration of the letter CH. A Kabbalist who masters this vibration will achieve the ability to differentiate the clear from the unclear, to eliminate any unclarity, and to recognize and understand everything in its purest form. All that is meant by the term "purity of ideas" is expressed by this letter vibration.

Mental: By using this vibration, the spirit — the mental body — will learn to consciously perceive and understand all the languages of the universe, i.e., all the languages of the spheres and planes, in their utmost clarity, and will gain the ability not only to understand all spiritual beings, men and animals, but also to be understood by them as well. That it will thereby be easy to understand all symbols existing in the universe goes without saying.

Astral: Astrally, the Kabbalist will attain, with the help of this letter vibration, the ability to understand and to practically apply rhythm in the macro- and microcosm in all its phases. By this he achieves power over the life and death of every being in all spheres and planes. If it is desirable, the Kabbalist may bring the dead back to life again or revive any decayed plant since the secret of rhythm, i.e., the secret of life, has been revealed to him by this letter vibration. Applying the same letter vibration, he may, of course, also make use of the opposite rhythm and cause immediate decay; for instance, to make a fully blooming tree wither within a few minutes, and so on. Even the Bible mentions a miracle by which Christ made a tree wither within a few moments as a sign of His might. The Kabbalist knows that such a miracle can only be caused by the power of the Word.

Matter: In the material world, this letter vibration is analogous to the Water element. It bestows on the Kabbalist the ability to recognize all the mysteries of the Water element and the magnetic fluids in all their analogies, and to control them at his discretion. Through this letter vibration the Kabbalist will bring the Water element on our earth under his will at his own discretion. If he so wishes, he can bring forth water everywhere; he can calm the waves of the sea, walk over the water, make rain showers cease, or cause rain; he can become absolute master of all the Water spirits and can achieve many other things.

I

Akasha: In the Akasha principle, this letter vibration is subject to destiny — to karmic law, which is the law of cause and effect. All doings and all actions, all life, come under this letter vibration. Likewise, the evolutionary law of all created things is expressed by it. At the same time, Divine Providence in Its most subtle form is manifested in this letter vibration. I is the tenth letter of the alphabet, and the number 10 represents the number 1 in its highest form in the Akasha principle.

Mental: In the mental body, this letter vibration is analogous to memory, remembrance and conscience. With the I vibration, the rhythm of 10, the Kabbalist is able to stimulate everything at his discretion, and thus control it completely. At the same time, he achieves the spiritual ability to call forth any remembrance in his memory or the memory of someone else, and furthermore to sharpen or weaken the conscience of a human being, the subtlest form of Divine Providence, depending in each case on what the Kabbalist intends to achieve with the help of this letter vibration. In short: all abilities regarding memory and conscience in the mental plane may be comprehended and controlled by this letter vibration.

Astral: In the astral kingdom, this letter vibration corresponds to the astral matrix with all its functions. As you know, the astral matrix is the connecting link between the material body and the soul or astral body: it is the so-called principle of life. It is also known that the astral matrix, and with it the whole astral body, is kept alive by breathing. With the help of this letter vibration, the Kabbalist is also in a position to completely control the breath with all its aspects and methods of application. With this letter vibration he is likewise able to restore the breath to a body that is already dead by banishing the astral matrix back into the dead body and by reuniting body and soul. After this, it will be easy for him to bind the desired spirit or mental body to the matter and to restore the person to life again.

Matter: In the material world, this letter vibration corresponds to all laws of analogies between the micro- and macrocosm. Everything that has shape, measure, number and weight has come into being with the help of this letter vibration. If the Kabbalist can control this letter vibration, he will be able to call forth the greatest miracles in the material world by using the respective analogies to shape, measure, number and weight. As one can see, shape, measure, number and weight are the chief components of the material world, and by bringing this letter vibration under his control the Kabbalist becomes their absolute master. It stands to reason that he will also be able to become a perfect metaphysician, and furthermore to comprehend all laws still presently unknown to our physical world, and to apply them as he pleases in all fields.

J

Akasha: In the Akasha principle, the J vibration is the vibration of the highest, most all-encompassing love, that is, of cosmic love. The J vibration enables the Kabbalist to comprehend and feel this love, which is one of the highest divine virtues, in all its aspects, in the microcosm as well as the macrocosm.

Mental: Mentally this letter vibration expresses the mystery of rapture or ecstasy in its highest form. This vibration allows one to comprehend, master and call forth at will the mystery of all four forms of ecstasy that are analogous to the elements. If the Kabbalist masters this letter vibration, he is able to call forth any ecstasy, especially ecstasies that are analogous to love, the Water element. It should be noted, however, that an ecstasy called forth

Kabbalistically has nothing to do with a hypnotic ecstasy or with a state of trance, which usually serves somnambulistic purposes. In this case, we speak of the ecstasy of one or several attributes of the spirit. Thus there exists, for instance, an ecstasy of will, of intellect (most enlightened intellect), of love and of consciousness. By the vibration of the letter J, two of these conditions at once — if necessary even all four of them — may be called forth at the discretion of the Kabbalist, either in his own or in somebody else's spirit. A state in which all four elements are equally brought into the highest form of ecstasy can hardly be comprehensible to a non-initiate and cannot be described with mere words.

Astral: This letter vibration is analogous to all laws of sympathy and attractive force in the astral world. It helps one to achieve the ability to master, call forth or diminish love and sympathy at one's discretion, in human beings as well as in animals. All the mysteries of love magic relating to man, beings and deities are revealed to the Kabbalist who masters this letter vibration.

Matter: In the material world, this letter vibration corresponds to the progenitive act of man and animal. The Kabbalist who masters this letter vibration in the material body will be able to call forth sexual desire in man and animal, and to increase it; he will also be able to predetermine and to influence the sex of an expected child, and above that to incorporate all the desired qualities in the child at the moment of the sexual act. Many other mysteries of love in their highest and lowest form, in all phases and spheres, are revealed to the Kabbalist who masters the vibration of this letter.

K

Akasha: In the Akasha principle, the vibration of the letter K is the vibration of omnipotence, which is also one of the divine virtues. There, omnipotence manifests itself as the highest power imaginable. To the Kabbalist who masters this vibration, this virtue will reveal itself as the all-encompassing power with which he will be able to work direct miracles in the micro- as well as the macrocosm. This virtue is manifested in the Akasha principle as the highest and purest light, which is analogous to the prime Fire principle.

Mental: In the mental world, this letter vibration corresponds to the state of manifestation of belief. The Kabbalist who is able to call forth the vibration of the letter K in the mental body will achieve a state of manifestation in which any thought, any wish, will at once become a reality in whichever plane the Kabbalist wishes it to be realized.

Astral: In the astral body, this letter vibration calls forth the virtue of courage with all its aspects, such as endurance, tenacity, etc. The Kabbalist is able to summon up a great degree of courage within himself and in other people, and to overcome and remove any feeling of fear within himself or his fellow man, just as he pleases. If he so wishes, he may also call forth and strengthen the instinct of self-preservation, either within himself or in others; and many other abilities that are analogous to courage — for instance perseverance, patience, etc. — may also be attained through this letter vibration.

Matter: In the material world, this letter vibration will call forth the ability to become absolute master of all earthly treasures. The Kabbalist who masters this letter vibration in the material world will get everything he wants effortlessly, whether for himself or for his fellow man.

L

Akasha: In the Akasha principle, this letter vibration represents the highest divine virtues that may be described in words, of whatever sort they may be. The Kabbalist ordinarily uses this letter vibration only when he wishes to comprehend the Divine

Majesty or the greatness of God in the form of the purest virtues. With the help of this vibration he will recognize how divine virtues work in the various spheres. It is impossible to enumerate all the divine virtues analogous to the L vibration, for their greatness, purity and profundity cannot be described, but only felt.

Mental: With the L vibration the Kabbalist will achieve, in his mental body, the ability to comprehend true morality in the spiritual sense, as seen from the Hermetic point of view. He will soon be convinced that good and evil, positive and negative moral attributes, must exist in order to be distinguished from each other. This vibration will call forth an enlightenment in the Kabbalist which will lead him to the borders of saintliness.

Astral: In the astral body, the mystery of magical equilibrium with regard to the character of any human being will be revealed to the Kabbalist with the help of this vibration. At the same time, the Kabbalist will attain the ability to spiritualize his astral body to such a degree that he will become one with all divine virtues. The mystery of astral invisibility completely reveals itself to him since, with the help of this vibration, he becomes a master over the astral light. If he so wishes, his astral body will become untouchable and will not be subject to influences by the elements, which means that the Kabbalist has reached the degree of astral immortality.

Matter: In the material world, the Kabbalist will gain perfect health, beauty and harmony, and will become absolute master of his own vitality through this letter vibration. He will be able to give his body permanent youth and appeal. If he so wishes and if he has permission from Divine Providence, he may apply this letter vibration successfully on others as well. The Kabbalist may connect any vital energy controlled by the L vibration to another letter vibration, and thus intensify it in a way that will allow him, if he so wishes, to incorporate it into a fluid condenser and thus work miracles in the art of healing. It stands to reason that in so doing he will also learn how to charge remedies and load fluid condensers Kabbalistically, and how to apply them, which means that he will be endowed with the ability to change any disharmony into harmony.

M

Akasha: In the Akasha principle, this letter vibration is analogous to the Prime Water Principle. Divine Providence has created water, the principle of fluids, in all its forms of existence in its prime principle up to its realization in the material world, with the help of the M vibration. The Kabbalist learns to fully comprehend, recognize and control the prime Water principle from the viewpoint of creation with the help of this letter vibration in the Akasha.

Mental: Since, in the mental kingdom or mental body, the prime Water principle is manifested as life, feeling and sentience, the Kabbalist, by mastering the M vibration, is given the mental ability to become complete master of his feelings, sentience, and life spirit. This ability also enables him to explore and control, in the spirit and with his own consciousness, the life, feelings and sentience of any other person.

Astral: The vibration of the letter M helps the Kabbalist to comprehend and master the astral Water element in all the spheres of activity of the astral world. At the same time, the Kabbalist thereby becomes absolute master of the pure magnetic fluid, which is analogous to the Water element — which is to say that the source of the magnetic fluid is the prime Water principle.

Matter: In the material world, the vibration of the letter M bestows on the Kabbalist the power of controlling the fluid principle in the whole world, in the micro- as well as in the macrocosm. Not only is the Kabbalist able to comprehend, with his consciousness, everything liquid in its prime principle, but he becomes an absolute master of it. This ability, when acquired through this vibration, also makes him master of the magnetic fluid and of everything connected with it. Thus, for instance, he may if he pleases control the laws of gravitation and many other things.

N

Akasha: In the Akasha principle, the highest state of blissfulness may be called forth by the mastery of this letter vibration, so that the Kabbalist is actually able to transfer himself, so to speak, into the seventh heaven. In this state of blissfulness, all the virtues, sentience, etc., that have reference to the material, astral and mental worlds are eliminated, and the Kabbalist experiences the supreme blissfulness which cannot be described in words.

Mental: In the mental body, this letter vibration corresponds to the mental matrix and to the mental aura as well. The mental matrix is the spiritual bonding agent which unites the astral body to the mental body and thus to the spirit. The mastery of this letter vibration will unveil to the Kabbalist all the mysteries relating to the mental matrix and bestow upon him the ability to comprehend, see, perceive and control the mental matrix in its sphere of activity, whether in regards to himself or others. The Kabbalist is also able to see his own mental aura or that of other people and to define it in its sphere of activity. He recognizes his own mental maturity and that of other people, and thus the degree of development of any spirit. He is given the ability to know exactly in which degree of density the spirit of a man, with his astral body, will dwell in the astral kingdom after his departure. Furthermore, the mastery of this letter vibration furnishes him with the ability to enlighten any man whom he deems worthy, in accordance with his maturity, by transferring the letter vibration upon him so that the person concerned is able to solve any problem corresponding to his degree of development without difficulty. It stands to reason that the Kabbalist is able, if he so wishes, to see through and master any spirit, via the aura or the mental matrix, in our material world as well as in the astral kingdom.

Astral: This letter vibration calls forth the instinct of self-preservation in the astral body of the astral world, which retains the astral body in the zone girdling the earth and makes it dependent upon the sphere of activity of the elements in the astral world. Through this letter vibration the Kabbalist attains the ability to bring the instinct of self-preservation in the astral world completely under his dominion, so that he cannot be attacked by any element in the astral world. This ability is especially appreciated by those magicians who are in the astral plane with their astral bodies, enjoying a state of absolute freedom and independence in the astral world which enables them to contact the genii or principals in the zone girdling the earth without having to first identify themselves with the astral emanations of these genii. Since they can never be influenced, whether in a positive or negative sense, by any principal of the zone girdling the earth, magicians who master this letter vibration perfectly and who, by virtue of their abilities, enjoy absolute freedom in the astral world are held in high esteem by all the principals. Such magicians are absolute masters of all beings in the zone girdling the earth and need not identify themselves with any prime attribute or any divine idea.

Matter: In the material world, everything related to the gait and movement of all human beings and animals is influenced by this letter vibration. If the Kabbalist masters this vibration, he becomes absolute master of all people and animals on our earth, and the gait and movement of all men and animals comes under his power. This is to say that the Kabbalist may, for example, make lame persons healthy and able to walk again. In our microcosm, in the entire material world, in all planes and worlds of the created cosmos, this letter vibration is identical to cohesion or the power of coherence, and therefore has a certain connection to specific gravity and the attractive power of everything material. As regards gravitation and the attractive power of matter, the vibration of the letter N, like that of M, makes the Kabbalist gain mastery over the laws of the power of coherence in any material thing.

O

Akasha: In the Akasha principle, the vibration of the letter O is the vibration of justice as a prime principle, as adherence to lawfulness, as acknowledgment, and as the honoring of the divine laws. The Kabbalist who calls forth and identifies himself with the O vibration in the Akasha principle attains divine justice. He will never do anything unjust and will never yield, for if he has reached this point he is completely filled with the lawfulness of Divine Providence and completely influenced by absolute justice. Wherever one deals with the principle of justice, it is controlled by the vibration of the letter O.

Mental: In the mental world, the vibration of the letter O gives expression to the absolute lawfulness of harmony in all four fundamental attributes of the spirit, and to its destiny, which is a contributory determinant in all future incarnations. By the mastery of the O vibration in the mental body, the Kabbalist attains a high level of judgment and the ability to comprehend, spiritually, any lawfulness, any intervention by Divine Providence, from the standpoint of justice. Having become incarnate justice himself by the vibration of the letter O, the Kabbalist who has proceeded thus far will never condemn anyone unjustly.

Astral: This vibration calls forth absolute astral contentment and equilibration in the astral body and bestows upon the Kabbalist the power to call forth, by Kabbalah, any situation in the astral world — without being made responsible for it by fate in any sense — which then will have its effect, either on the Akasha principle in the mental world, in the spirit, on the astral world or astral body, or on the material world, just as the Kabbalist wishes. Since the Kabbalist has now become incarnate justice himself, he will never bring about unfavorable situations in any sphere without the strict order of Divine Providence. Fate has no influence on the Kabbalist who has developed to this point, and he must justify himself only before Divine Providence. This letter vibration gives the Kabbalist a sense of contentment, absolute security, infallibility and irreproachableness.

Matter: This vibration will call forth situations in the material world which will bring about absolute success and good fortune in every respect. The Kabbalist mastering this vibration learns to understand, and eventually to control completely, the working and functioning of the electromagnetic fluids in the human body and the material world in their relation to the higher spheres. On the basis of this ability, the Kabbalist will become a perfect master of astrophysics and metaphysics.

P

Akasha: In the Akasha principle, this letter vibration calls forth a longing for spiritual progress, spiritual perfection, and the highest spiritualization. The highest form of expression of the law of evolution of any spirit is embodied in it. The Kabbalist who, through this letter vibration, is urged in the Akasha principle to aspire towards the Divine Light will sense a profound, ever increasing longing for unification with the four fundamental divine attributes, and will realize how that deeply divine love which is present in every human being constantly urges him on towards connection with divine omnipotence, love and wisdom, and towards the incorporation of these qualities within himself. The yearning for divine unification with the four fundamental divine attributes is a specific sentience which is only comprehensible to the practitioner and which one may experience but never describe.

Mental: In the mental body, this vibration calls forth a deep religious sentience, one of devotion towards the highest infinity, which is, however, also expressed through a deep humility of the spirit. The more deeply and frequently the Kabbalist is permeated with this letter vibration, the deeper will be his feeling of humility, and it is in this state that he will comprehend the greatest and most powerful proximity of the divine majesty, of Divine Providence. At the same time, he will have the feeling that by this most profound humility he is nearest to omnipotence, universal love, omniscience and omnipresence. He will be fully aware of the fact that, as a faithful servant of Divine Providence, he is only able to express his thoughts by giving assistance, at any time, to suffering humankind and to those who still struggle severely with their fates, and to help — not only materially but, above all, spiritually — the spirits of all those who strive upwards.

Astral: In the astral body, this letter vibration calls forth the yearning to ennoble and transform one's character, and the longing for magical equilibrium. Furthermore, it calls forth the ability to perceive beauty from the universal standpoint as the consequence of perfect harmony. Only the honestly aspiring Kabbalist can experience the true essence of beauty without being bound by outside appearance, which is usually only relative. The feeling of absolute beauty and harmony in their absolute purity and profundity can only be achieved by the mastery of this letter vibration.

Matter: In the material world, this letter vibration is parallel to the vibration of some of the other letters which are identical with the procreative instinct. It has no direct specific analogies; instead, it has a particular analogous connection to love for children, to maternal love. As soon as the Kabbalist masters this vibration materially, he will be able to achieve, in the material world, everything relating to the procreative instinct, to maternal love, love for children, and many other things.

QU

Phonetically, QU is a combination of K and W and is therefore not regarded as an individual letter. In the Hebrew Kabbalah, the pronunciation of QU is identical with that of K and must therefore be dealt with in the same way. From the Kabbalistic point of view, however, the letter QU is not to be regarded as an individual letter with any analogies of its own.

R

Akasha: In the Akasha principle, this letter vibration, together with some others, is attributed to independence and freedom. The Kabbalist who calls forth this letter vibration in the Akasha will become guardian and master of freedom and independence. In this state he feels internally perfect; he feels free of any oppressive burden of law, for by the mastery of all the preceding letters he has achieved a degree of maturity through which his feeling of independence has been transformed into an absolute state of security and irreproachableness.

Mental: The mastery of this letter vibration in the mental body allows the Kabbalist to acquire an excellent intellect and, furthermore, the feeling of freedom of will and freedom of action; he acquires not only this, but also the degree of maturity through which he will never violate any law, having himself become master of all laws. Any law transferred into the micro- or macrocosm is personified by him and must serve him. This feeling of absolute security cannot be explained in words. The Kabbalist who has proceeded to this point will first convince himself of what has been said and, in spite of his freedom of will, he shall choose to subject himself willingly to Divine Providence and accept missions to serve Divine Providence with deep humility, immense gratitude and the highest devotion, all without losing his feeling of absolute freedom of will in any way.

Astral: Calling forth this letter vibration in the astral body will awaken a geniality which will manifest itself in a number of abilities. Anything which a spirit trained in this way may undertake in an astral body endowed with the same abilities is equipped with a high degree of geniality of which a non-initiate cannot have the faintest idea.

Matter: In the physical world, this letter vibration will cause an broadening of the Kabbalist's intellect which will enable him to comprehend any knowledge quickly and without difficulty, and also to express his knowledge in words. By so doing, the Kabbalist will acquire any abilities he may need to carry out any mission he accepts.

S

Akasha: In the Akasha principle, the S vibration represents the all-permeating power and all-encompassing power — in contrast and comparison to the K, which represents omnipotence. The letter S is thus the quantitative form (in contrast to the qualitative form as embodied in the letter K) of the first prime principle of the highest divine attributes. The S as an all-encompassing power is to be understood substantially, whereas the K must be valued as the highest divine virtue. One who is able to call forth the S vibration in the Kabbalistic manner in the Akasha principle will come into contact with the most subtle substance of the divine being, the primordial divine Fire. This primordial divine Fire is active as a substantial power in everything that has been created by Divine Providence. Omnipotence, on the other hand, expresses itself in the prime idea as the prime virtue of the first divine principle in all the kingdoms and in everything that has been created. Therefore, in all cases wherein the realization of the primordial divine Fire, the all-encompassing power, is the point in question, the S vibration is to be used rather than the K.

Mental: On applying this vibration in the mental body, the Kabbalist will attain the spiritual gift of complete mastery over the electrical fluid. The Kabbalist will thereby understand, and be able to control, everything that is analogous to the electrical fluid or Fire principle.

Astral: In the astral body, this letter vibration will call forth absolute clairvoyance in its purest form in all spheres and planes of creation. At the same time, the Kabbalist is given the gift of prophecy, by which the ability to see across time and space is meant; furthermore, he will attain complete might over all human beings and animals, along with many other abilities that are analogous to this vibration.

Matter: In the material world, mastery over this vibration brings mastery over the Kabbalist's own consciousness in itself, as well as over the consciousness of all human beings and entities of all spheres and planes of our macrocosm, beginning with the kingdom of the elements and extending to the highest beings, such as angels, primary beings, genii and so forth. It stands to reason that, along with the gift of transferring consciousness, other magical abilities may be developed at the same time.

SCH (SH)

While describing the S vibration, I mentioned that the letter K stands for omnipotence — for the primordial Light — and that S stands for the primordial Fire. The vibration of the letter SCH connects the primordial Light and primordial Fire and thus indicates the unmanifested omnipotence. The SCH vibration therefore represents the primordial principle which is superior to K and S. The SCH is the letter with which Divine Providence represents the primordial principle of Fire and the primordial

Light of unmanifest omnipotence. The SCH vibration thus indicates, so to speak, the first outpouring of divine creation, and is therefore regarded as the highest letter, while the S and K, in their manifestation, are subject to this mother letter.

It is pointed out in Kabbalah that Divine Providence has created the primordial principle of the elements by the three letters A, SCH and M, and that all other letters originated from these fundamental letters. According to Kabbalistic lawfulness, the A is analogous to the primordial element of the Air principle, the SCH to the primordial Fire, and the M to the primordial Water element. The A is analogous to intellect, wisdom, the lawfulness of equilibrium, and so on; the SCH to the will, the all-encompassing power and omnipotence; and the M to love. SCH as a primordial principle is the principle of activity that is analogous to the electrical fluid; the letter M, as its opposite, is the principle of the primordial Water element that is analogous to the magnetic fluid. For reasons of balance, the A plays a mediating role between primordial Fire and primordial Water. Thus it should be noted that the SCH vibration represents the primordial element of Fire, the M vibration the primordial element of Water, and that the A vibration mediates between the two. Consequently, these three letters are the primordial or fundamental letters, the "mother letters."

These brief remarks are necessary in order to explain the actual position of the vibration of the letter SCH and in order to avoid any confusion in the use of this vibration. Originating from these three letters, further letters and their special effects came into existence, as I have already explained.

Akasha: Whoever is able to call forth this letter in the Akasha principle will recognize, from the Akasha, the primordial element of Fire together with the primordial Light and acquire the highest form of enlightenment. Symbolically, the SCH appears as a shining sun in the Akasha principle, with the primordial Fire, as substance, at its center and the primordial Light as the emission of the primordial Fire. This is also the case in normal creation, wherein the sun, as a primordial fire, signifies a glowing heat, and the emission of the fire of the sun is considered as light. It would be possible to mention numerous analogies between symbols and letter vibrations with regard to their primordial universal qualities, but these hints will be sufficient for the practical Kabbalist.

Mental: In the mental body of the Kabbalist, this letter vibration will bring about the highest enlightenment, the highest spiritualization, which increases to the point of ecstasy. This ecstasy is a positive form of rapture and only a little different from the one described with regard to the letter J. The J vibration contains the primordial principle of love; the SCH vibration, on the other hand, is the principle of the primordial Fire. Through the SCH vibration the intellect is also enlightened to a certain extent; no less so is consciousness, so that both become more receptive.

Astral: In the astral body, the SCH vibration calls forth the primordial state of the manifestation of belief and likewise the ability to transmute and perfectly master the Fire element in all kingdoms. Since the principle of the will is also identical to this letter vibration in the astral world, it naturally also comes to bear therein.

Matter: In his material body, the Kabbalist will fortify his absolute belief with the help of this vibration. He will learn to master the electrical fluid in all three kingdoms (to a larger extent in the material world), and at the same time acquire the ability to influence everything in the material world with the help of the electrical fluid or the Fire element, wherever an analogous application is possible.

T

Akasha: In the Akasha principle, this letter vibration awakens a high inspiration which has special reference to all the lawfulness of this principle. A Kabbalist endowed with this gift in the Akasha principle will, with the help of the T vibration, perceive the reception of divine inspiration and intuition regarding everything that attracts his interest and attention.

Mental: In the mental body, this letter vibration awakens remarkable inventive abilities which are especially favorable with regard to those things that are of special interest. This gift also favorably influences one's memory, especially one's mechanical memory.

Astral: This letter vibration enables the astral body to carry out true astral magic in its complete scope. Since this ability is, at the same time, also connected with mastery over all the elements, the Kabbalist is given other great advantages which he will certainly appreciate and value accordingly.

Matter: In the material body and the material world, this letter vibration enables the Kabbalist to comprehend fully, and make practical use of, all the laws of analogy in the three kingdoms — mineral, vegetable and animal.

U

Akasha: The vibration of the letter U in the Akasha principle bestows upon the Kabbalist the ability to comprehend this principle in the act of creation and from the point of view of karma. If the Kabbalist masters this vibration (and with repeated practice he will do so), the primordial existence of all that exists in all its forms will be revealed to him so that he will fully comprehend it and so that it will become acquainted with his consciousness. This attribute and gift cannot be acquired by anything other than the vibration of the letter U.

Mental: The U vibration calls forth the highest form of intuition and inspiration in the mental body, and at the same time renders it possible for the Kabbalist to explore and master his own karma and its changes.

Astral: When mastering the U vibration in the astral body, the Kabbalist will attain the ability to transfer his consciousness wherever he pleases, and thus to become a perfect master over his consciousness. At the same time, he will gain the ability to call forth states of trance of any kind, just as he pleases, and to completely master the art of astral travel.

Matter: In the material world, this letter vibration enables one to understand and apply the mysteries of the Akasha principle regarding matter, and imparts the ability to comprehend the sphere of activity of the tetrapolar magnet with regard to all matter, to master it and to penetrate into all its mysteries. Among other things, the Kabbalist also learns, with the help of this vibration, to Kabbalistically apply the principle of the ether in our material world from the magical point of view.

V

From the Kabbalistic point of view, the letter V is not an actual letter and is usually dealt with in the same way as F, which has the same phonetic pronunciation. If pronounced softly it is almost a W, and if pronounced sharply it is phonetically equivalent to F. Therefore, there are no correspondences to V. The description of W follows.

W

Akasha: In the Akasha principle, the W vibration will call forth cosmic unification of consciousness and cosmic inspiration of consciousness, or, regarded Kabbalistically, cosmic intuition. Seen from a higher cosmic point of view, this letter vibration is also an aspect of cosmic universal love. Divine Providence will allow only the Kabbalist who is able to call forth the W vibration in the Akasha principle to comprehend and understand the primordial principle of cosmic intuition — which at the same time may be regarded as the outpouring of cosmic love — in its complete scope. The Kabbalist must experience this, for the effects of this vibration in the Akasha principle cannot be expressed in words.

Mental: This letter vibration will awaken all potential mediumistic abilities within the mental kingdom or mental body of the Kabbalist. Amongst many other things, the Kabbalist will, for instance, develop excellent clairsentience, and will be able to influence his spirit with any idea in any field of science in such a way as to identify himself with that idea. At the same time, this letter vibration increases one's ability of concentration up to the highest possible state, called *samadhi* in India. Whoever is unable to concentrate efficiently in Kabbalah, or who easily becomes tired and exhausted when performing Kabbalistic concentration exercises, should apply this letter vibration. He will soon discover that, when applying the concentration exercises of the three senses for a longer period, neither mental, nor astral, nor physical weariness or exhaustion will arise.

Astral: In the astral body, this vibration will awaken the religious feeling which is necessary for true mysticism. Furthermore, it will also awaken the necessary disposition for this. If desired, the astral body is able to call forth a temple atmosphere within itself or in its vicinity whenever and wherever it is needed. Naturally, those who are in the vicinity of the Kabbalist will be seized by a religious and mystical reverence which passes over into some sort of rapture and detachment from the world. By calling forth this letter vibration repeatedly, an absolute facility for clairaudience and speaking over large distances will develop. The Kabbalist will not only be able to hear all beings and perceive, with his sense of hearing, everything spoken in the remotest past, in the present or in the future, but he will also clearly perceive, over the greatest distances, everything to which he directs his consciousness; and, functioning as a transmitter, he will be able to speak words into his astral body that will be heard physically even over a great distance by non-initiates. This means that the Kabbalist is thus capable of condensing his astral sounds in such a way that the words may not only be heard but also recorded on discs or any other recording equipment over any distance, if the Kabbalist so wishes and without the necessity of his physical presence. Of course, this ability will be acquired only by a true Kabbalist who has honestly struggled through to this point.

Matter: In the material body, the Kabbalist may, with the help of this letter vibration, acquire the ability to distinguish the transitory from the eternal or universal here in our physical world. The Kabbalist will understand everything relative on our earth and be able to bring it under his control and make use of it. He will at once recognize any kind of glamor or illusion in all beings, whether human or animal, but will also be able to call forth the same in a man or an animal. Since this letter vibration has a specific connection to the Water element, the control of that element on our earth is conferred upon the Kabbalist at the same time. Many abilities which are analogous to Water and the magnetic fluid and which may be made use of in the material world will be bestowed on the Kabbalist as a reward for his work. Amongst other things, there is, for instance, the ability to magnetize in the healing art or the art to call forth water instantaneously in extreme heat and drought, to materialize or dematerialize water, turn it into ice, and so on.

X

Like V, this is not an independent letter from the Kabbalistic point of view, but a combination of I, K and S, and must therefore be regarded as such. Thus the X has no Kabbalistic connections, and no analogous description of the letter is possible.

Y-Ü (UE)

Akasha: The true source of the rhythm of life and its purpose will be revealed to one who masters this letter vibration in the Akasha principle. From the beginning of creation, this letter vibration has been influencing the law of evolution towards its perfection. Since this vibration is difficult to understand, only the experienced Kabbalist who has reached this point in his scientific work will succeed in fully comprehending and mastering the primordial rhythms of life and the laws of harmony (lawfulness).

Mental: In the mental or spiritual plane, this vibration, like the one previously discussed, will bring about the profoundest cosmic intuition and inspiration, which, at the same time, may be regarded as the gift of absolute devotion to and deepest love for Divine Providence. Another advantage in working with this vibration lies in the fact that many other abilities (which cannot be expressed in mere words since they can only be evaluated macrocosmically) may develop out of this mental ability.

Astral: Mastered in the astral body, this letter vibration will impart an aptitude for prophecy so excellent that it will exclude any possibility of error. He who has become familiar with this vibration will have spiritualized his astral body in such a way that he will be able to see and know prophetically, beyond all doubt, the destiny of everything — of every creature, whether man or animal — from the microcosmic point of view. His prophecies will be as certain and infallible as if they came directly from Divine Providence. Such a high degree of prophetic ability cannot be acquired through any other letter vibration. The greatest prophets that ever lived acquired their prophetic abilities only in the secret schools of prophecy in which true Kabbalah was taught.

Matter: When called forth in the material body, this letter vibration will lead to the ability to explore, comprehend and apply the absolute effectiveness of the Akasha principle in the material world with regard to all forms and bodies in the mineral, vegetable, animal and human kingdoms. At the same time, the ability to make astral and material objects invisible is also achieved with the help of this letter vibration, for whoever recognizes and masters the Akasha principle in the material world in all its forms of existence is able to change the degree of density in our material world at his discretion. Thus the Kabbalist possessing this ability is in a position to dematerialize his body and to materialize it again at a great distance within a few moments. Consequently he is able to bridge time and space over any distance, not only mentally and astrally but materially. The Kabbalist may acquire many other magical abilities if he has succeeded in bringing this letter vibration under his control. Many of the miracles cited in the Bible, and which have been worked by initiates throughout the ages, confirm that what is written here is the truth.

Z

Akasha: To call forth the Z vibration in the Akasha principle is to influence the higher intellectual power, especially with regard to the process we call cognition. This ability, awakened to a high degree, is in accordance with all the universal laws of the microcosm and the macrocosm. Of course, this ability expresses itself in all forms of consciousness and reaches its full potential Kabbalistically.

Mental: In the mental world or the spirit, this letter vibration will bring about a general increase of intellectual talents and abilities of whatever kind. It especially bestows the ability to recollect all memories of previous incarnations. But this is not all: Apart from this, the Kabbalist is also endowed with the ability to recover, in his present incarnation, all the intellectual gifts and talents he may have acquired in his former lives. He will suddenly become aware that, in actuality, no time has elapsed between his former embodiments and his present incarnation — which means that he is not conscious of time and space. He has the impression that he has lived through his thousands of incarnations in a very short time. All the abilities he once possessed are suddenly re-awakened within him. He can use all the languages he once mastered, at his discretion, without having to learn them again. In a word, the Kabbalist has, with the help of this letter vibration, attained the ability to adapt himself to any situation in such a way that he will not cause chaos within himself even if he becomes aware of all his former incarnations. Those magicians, however, who wish to learn about their former incarnations without having properly prepared themselves usually have to struggle hard to adapt themselves to the given situation. The feeling of being responsible for evil deeds will arise and find expression in serious remorse. Apart from this, the retrospection into former incarnations without appropriate preparation will call forth a feeling of dependence on destiny, and a limited freedom of will in thought and deed will make itself known. It may also happen to an unprepared magician that, as a result of this retrospection, he will be shocked by his actual age, and thus it will be a severe hindrance to his actions because of his inability to imagine himself as youthful. Such disadvantages, however, will only befall magicians and other people who have not been adequately trained. A Kabbalist who has worked through to this point and who genuinely masters the Z vibration need fear nothing of the sort.

Astral: In the astral body, the Z vibration will call forth all kinds of artistic abilities, especially those which are particularly desirable to the Kabbalist. Likewise, the ability to put any abstract idea into easily comprehensible terms will develop. Furthermore, this vibration makes it possible for the Kabbalist to send and receive messages through the air. True initiates of the Orient who deal with high Tantric magic and who also attain practical mastery of the Z vibration possess the ability to exchange messages with the help of the Air principle. This ability must not be confused with the ordinary telepathy familiar to us, in which thoughts are only linked with other thoughts when one spirit speaks to the other. The ability to send messages through the air with the help of the Z vibration is a very different process, for here the Air principle is used as a conductor for the sound vibration, which is quite another thing than that which is generally understood as telepathy.

Matter: This vibration will make the body tenacious in a material sense and will furnish it with immense endurance. For instance, the Kabbalist may undertake long trips on foot without getting the least bit tired. The Kabbalist who finds it desirable to direct his concentration to the material world is, with the help of this letter vibration, able to prepare his body in a manner which will allow him to walk many miles without feeling any fatigue, exhaustion or any of the other attendant side-effects of a long march. In Tibet there are so-called "runners" who cover hundreds of miles by leaps without getting tired and who achieve this with the help of Tantric formulas which have a certain analogous connection to this Z vibration. Many other abilities will be imparted to the material body by the Z vibration: for instance, controlling storms, calling them forth and calming them down, changing the direction of the winds, etc. Since the Z vibration is analogous to cheerfulness and all relevant qualities such as gaiety, amusement, and so on, the Kabbalist need only conduct the Z vibration into himself or his surroundings and he will instantaneously make the saddest gathering change over to amusing thoughts, putting people into the best humor.

Although the Z is the last letter of our alphabet, I shall describe two more letters, the Ä and Ö, which, for certain reasons, I have left until the end.

Ä (AE)

Akasha: If the Kabbalist calls forth the Ä vibration in the Akasha principle, it will be possible for him to know the source and the mystery of life and death and their transformation. He will become once more convinced that, in reality, death does not exist, for our so-called death is but a transformation from one state into another. The Kabbalist will also be enlightened by the Ä vibration in the Akasha principle concerning the cause of this transformation and all its connections. Likewise, he will also become acquainted with, and learn to master, all negative beings in all spheres and planes with regard to their sphere of activity. The purpose for which negative beings have been created will become absolutely clear to him. Since all beings are equal in the primordial principle, each having been created by Divine Providence to fulfill a particular task, there is no necessity to disguise the negative beings, for from the Kabbalist's point of view everything is pure. Here the adage: "To the pure, everything is pure," becomes relevant. If there were no negative beings it would be impossible, from the Hermetic point of view, to distinguish between good and evil; and if there were no passions, there would be no virtues either. This vibration confirms to the Kabbalist the words contained in the Bible: "Through night to light," the deep symbolic meaning of which will now become clear to him.

Mental: Mastering the Ä vibration in the mental body will impart the ability to see all thoughts, actions and wishes concerning matter, and to become their absolute master. This ability — as well as many others which the Kabbalist may achieve in the mental body with the help of the Ä vibration — has reference to physical matter at the same time, so that this vibration is assumed to be the most material one, even though we are concerned here with the control of Ä in the mental kingdom.

Astral: In the astral kingdom, the Ä vibration represents all the desires and passions, the inclination to self-satisfaction, etc.

Whoever masters this vibration in the astral body will become absolute master and ruler over all desires and passions. He is, furthermore, able to relinquish his attachment to mental, astral and material virtues and objects. This means complete independence and freedom for the Kabbalist, and the true meaning of the saying: "Bind yourself and you will be free," will thereby become intelligible to him.

Matter: Since the vibration of the letter Ä is one of the most physical vibrations — no matter whether it be called forth in the mental, the astral, the Akasha or the material world — the earth is influenced by it to an increased degree. With the help of this vibration, the Kabbalist attains the ability to recognize the most materialized components of our earth — irrespective of their being minerals, ores or the like — and to influence them Kabbalistically. Thus, with the help of this vibration, he will become absolute master of the physical matter on our planet.

Ö (OE)

Finally, here is the description of the letter Ö.

Akasha: In the Akasha principle, the Ö vibration calls forth the most profound cognition, which can only be experienced through love divine, along with the knowledge that is called the Kabbalistic quintessence. With the help of this vibration, the Kabbalist learns all the possibilities of transformation of the spirit, all the systems and ways serving this end, and all knowledge concerning transformation in all other fields. From all of this, he learns — beginning with the act of creation — what all forms of transformation had to endure in order to reunite. The Kabbalist must attain all the abilities that are offered by the Ö vibration in the Akasha principle, must seize all the possibilities, in order to be convinced that they cannot be described in words but must be experienced.

I have mentioned the letters Ä and Ö as the last ones in this series of exercises, because with the help of their vibrations one is able to comprehend, from the Akasha principle, the crown of all wisdom in the micro- and macrocosms from the act of creation to the present state of evolution and even to the final development.

Mental: Called forth in the mental kingdom, the Ö vibration will secure the perfect mastery of Kabbalistic alchemy. By this one should understand the transformation of ideas, virtues, etc., by the Kabbalistic word, which is a very great and comprehensive subject.

Astral: In the astral kingdom, the Ö vibration develops the ability of perfect astral projection and the mastery of all occult and magical phenomena that have reference to transformation, so that the Kabbalist may, for instance, assume any desired form in the astral body without being recognized by other beings — only Divine Providence is able to recognize him. Apart from this, the Kabbalist is able to transform any astral vibration into the vibration he chooses and to do the same with any element.

Matter: When mastered in the physical body, the Ö vibration will lead to perfect knowledge of Kabbalistic alchemy in the material world. The Kabbalist is taught the true preparation and charging of the philosopher's stone in the physical sense. As he can use the Kabbalah to influence, at will, any vibration — whether an atomic vibration or the vibrations of electrons — and as he is able to transform it into the vibration he desires, he will also naturally master the laws of transmutation perfectly. Therefore he is able to transform any metal into gold, any stone into a precious stone, etc., if he so wishes. With the help of this vibration the Kabbalist will be furnished with many other abilities which, at this point, he cannot even dream of, and which non-initiates would regard as absolutely impossible.

The description of the mystico-Kabbalistic use of the whole alphabet with special reference to each letter is herewith concluded. In the Hermetic Kabbalah this is called "the use of the one-letter key." At the same time Part II, or the study of practical letter mysticism, is also concluded. The Kabbalist has been taught to spell Kabbalistically, is now in unison with the micro- and the macrocosm, has acquired all the abilities necessary for further formula magic and, being prepared accordingly, may now proceed to the third part of the practice. Meanwhile, the Kabbalist has now come to the conclusion that this is quite a different kind of mysticism than that described in conventional books, and that the preparatory exercises for the practical Kabbalistic formula magic indicated in my first book, *Initiation into Hermetics,* have been unavoidably necessary; for without the acquired preliminary knowledge and abilities, no one is able to practice Kabbalistic formula magic.

The one-letter exercises described here serve the purpose of working, directly from the Akasha principle, upon the mental, astral and material worlds, of creating the causes directly in the causal world and bringing about their effects in the spirit (the mental plane), the astral (the astral plane) and the material world (the physical plane). The Kabbalistic use of each letter enables the Kabbalist to be effective — first, directly in the mental plane, later in the astral plane, and finally directly in the material world as well — without having to create causes in the Akasha principle in order to bring about the effects. When, by completing the whole series of letters, the Kabbalist has acquired all the abilities necessary for further Kabbalistic operations, he need not operate directly from the Akasha principle in his further use of those Kabbalistic formulas which are called, by initiates, "the cosmic language" — i.e., he need not put himself into the necessary state of trance, but can immediately bring about effects by words of power and work creatively and directly from any plane.

The abilities mentioned here are only a small part of those which the Kabbalist may acquire. It is impossible to specify all the abilities which may be acquired and attained by Kabbalistic mysticism, since (without exaggeration) they come near to the unutterable, the intellectually incomprehensible. It is therefore up to the Kabbalist to satisfy himself by means of his own systematic and practical labor.

Never before has so much information regarding the spheres of action been made public as is being done by me in this book, which should serve as an incentive for all aspiring Kabbalists and their work. One may regard the alphabetic sequence of letters as influences of the emanation of Divine Providence, indicating the way, starting from the lowest level of the physical world up to the highest level of unification with Divine Providence. With these twenty-two letters, which are regarded as the great arcana in Hermetic science, everything that exists in the micro- and the macrocosm, the miniature world and the universe, is present. The Kabbalist who has completed the exercises with the one-letter key will fully comprehend all this.

In the next chapter, the combined letters and their effects on the mental, astral and material worlds will be dealt with. These combined letters, however, are no longer to be used for exercises; they are assigned for immediate Kabbalistic work and effects.

PART III

THE PRACTICE OF FORMULA MAGIC

Step VIII
The Kabbalistic Alphabet
The Two-Letter Key

The one-letter key described in Step VII is the most important key in Kabbalah and serves the Kabbalist as a kind of preparation. It is called the one-letter key because it represents the number 1, this being the number of the deity. When meditating accordingly upon this, the Kabbalist will realize that he should make use of the one-letter key only for his personal development and that it is not advisable to work with single letters for others, since the single-letter key works directly from the causal sphere, the Akasha. Should the Kabbalist bring about effects for others directly from the causal sphere, he would not create any karma by so doing and would therefore be responsible for everything himself. If, on the other hand, he operates with several letters, the effects will not emanate from the causal world but (depending on the number of letters he uses Kabbalistically) from the mental, astral or material worlds, and the causes created will be recorded in the Akasha principle.

* Since the one-letter key emanates from the causal world, it is effective in the Akasha principle without actually creating any causes.

* The two-letter key creates causes of a mental nature, and therefore also causes mental effects.

* The use of the three-letter key brings about astral effects as a consequence; it creates certain situations in the astral, and its effects are therefore of an astral nature.

   *   Formulas with several letters used together create material causes, and thus bring about material effects, establishing the destiny or karma materially.

In the following section, I will describe the two-letter key — which no longer represents the preliminary micro- and macrocosmic mysticism but which already belongs to the subject of formula magic. The micro- and macrocosmic mysticism, being symbolic of Divine Providence, is signified only by the one-letter key.

When using the two-letter key, the Kabbalist works with two letters which may already be regarded as a formula, so that from now on the Kabbalist will be called a formula magician.

The two-letter key is identical with the mental plane and mental body or spirit. The practice of formula magic in the mental sphere requires the use of two letters; depending on the effect that is planned, one or another combination of letters will be chosen. The analogous key of a single letter also serves as a *leitmotiv* in this case. In combining letters, the idea is the basis; thus in Kabbalistic operations a certain combination of letters has quite a different significance than in any intellectual language. From the Kabbalist's point of view, the word "dog," for instance, does not simply denote the animal: it has quite another meaning. This has been noted only for the reader's information.

Now I will describe, in a few short words of instruction, the two-letter key and its effects on the mental plane. When working with this key the formula magician must first imagine, in his "I" consciousness, his astral and, finally, his mental body, just as he did when working with the one-letter key, and he must pronounce the two selected letters as a spirit. He must be aware that his physical organs of speech — his tongue, lips, larynx, etc. — do not utter those two letters in a Kabbalistic manner, but that this is done by his spirit. And, again as with the one-letter key, the concentration exercises of the three senses must be adhered to when pronouncing the two letters; this means that each letter must be uttered in a visual, acoustical and intuitive way. One begins with the first letter and then proceeds to the second one; as with the other keys, one may also proceed inductively or deductively with the two-letter key for one's own spirit or mental body. However, it is possible to apply this key for others, too, either directly to the relevant spirit or mental body if a direct influence is to be exerted, or to the mental plane in general (and there again either to one's own microcosm or to that of another human being), depending on the causes to be created with the help of the formula and the effects one wants to produce.

The Use of the Two-Letter Key With the Letter A

A-A

It has already been mentioned in connection with the description of the A that this letter is analogous to the Air principle and thus to reason and intellect in all their phases. Consequently, when applying the two-letter key in the mental sphere, the A-A will have a particularly strong influence on the intellect, whether used inductively or deductively and whether for oneself or for someone else. The formula magician will make use of the double letter A-A if he wishes or intends to awaken reminiscences, to enlighten the intellect, to strengthen the memory or to awaken other intellectual abilities.

A-B

If pronounced Kabbalistically, these two letters will heal mental diseases and remove depression, fear, etc., with the help of the electromagnetic fluid. In this case the formula magician need not imagine the electromagnetic fluid, for it will work automatically and indirectly by means of the concentration exercises of the three senses resulting from the Kabbalistic utterance. With the help of these two letters, the formula magician is also in a position to exert a healing influence on his own or on someone else's chest region and to treat any pectoral complaint Kabbalistically from the mental plane, particularly in such cases where the causes are mental ones, as for instance shortness of breath caused by states of anxiety, etc.

A-C

With the help of these two letters pronounced Kabbalistically, the formula magician is able to embody any idea, virtue, etc., at his discretion, either in a fluid or solid form of whatever kind, in a similar way as with a fluid condenser. In this state of development the Kabbalist no longer requires any recipes for the fabrication of fluid condensers, since he is now able to charge, by Kabbalah, any object, whether solid or fluid, with the desired virtue.

A-D

Uttered in a Kabbalistic manner, these two letters particularly strengthen the "I" consciousness and the entire mental matrix, meaning its emanation. These two letters are especially used by the formula magician when he wants to work over great distances, namely telepathically. The ability to work over a distance is considerably improved in the mental body by this formula.

A-E

This formula makes a transfer of consciousness easier. At the same time it makes it possible for the transferred consciousness to absorb bright and true impressions and to transfer these into the normal consciousness.

166

A-F

Applied Kabbalistically, the letters A-F will remove any instability, especially with regard to the intellect, and in particular will strengthen the four fundamental attributes of the spirit. Therefore, this formula is usually employed Kabbalistically in those cases where great intellectual exertion is involved, and where will, feeling and consciousness are overly fatigued by such exertion. The three basic attributes of will, feeling and consciousness are particularly strengthened and equilibrated by the use of this letter combination so that any fatigue will vanish.

A-G

Wherever an atmosphere of peace, tranquility and equilibration is desired, these two letters should be applied through the two-letter key. Inductively used for oneself, this formula will bring the blessing of Divine Providence. If forgiveness (intercession) is anywhere to be achieved for someone else, it will be done with the help of these two letters. Furthermore, this letter combination will bring about the immediate calming of any excitation of the human mind.

A-H

The influence of divine intuition on oneself and on others will be attained by this key. In particular, immature human beings who feel themselves surrounded by enemies, and therefore oppressed and persecuted, may be cured and freed by the Kabbalistic application of these two letters. Also, those who believe that an injustice has befallen them can be enlightened by this key so as to understand that everything that is done is done justly.

A-CH

This letter combination is a special formula with whose help one's memory may be considerably strengthened, long forgotten reminiscences may be recalled to mind, thoughts and ideas may be returned to one's consciousness, and many other things. Applied inductively for oneself, this key possesses the might to recall to the formula magician's mind the memories of his former incarnation as intensively as if he had experienced them yesterday.

A-I

This key is especially suitable to awaken a man's conscience. It is applicable in all cases of unjustified persecution, or where unscrupulous human beings and actions are involved. Applied to oneself, this formula will awaken high inspiration and pure intuition.

A-J

This two-letter key increases mental enthusiasm, irrespective of its purpose. When used for oneself, this formula will transform indifference into the opposite attribute; when used for others, it will awaken interest either for the formula magician himself or for a specific purpose.

A-K

This letter combination is used to eliminate any doubt within oneself or another. If one works with it inductively, it gives self-confidence. When applied deductively, it will call forth trust and confidence so that any doubts will be removed.

A-L

If someone has erred but does not want to admit it, or is ashamed of having made a mistake, the proper attitude will be conveyed to him with the help of this formula. Applied to oneself, the A-L combination will bring about a greater adaptability to any idea in the mental body.

A-M

Like the preceding formula, this one is also suitable for increasing one's adaptability, especially in cases where the mind predominates over feeling. This letter combination may also be successfully applied to people who, quite apart from their intellectual receptivity, should also act upon their feelings.

A-N

By using this formula, any listlessness within oneself and any intellectual fatigue in others may be eliminated. This two-letter key may particularly serve as a remedy after long physical and astral ailments that have caused mental fatigue and require a period of convalescence.

A-O

If someone has difficulties arriving at a conclusion or comprehending a particular kind of subject matter, the necessary enlightenment can be brought about by this formula. Also, in the event that someone has done something wrong, he may be Kabbalistically inspired to see his mistake. The person concerned will then quickly endeavor to right his wrongs.

A-P

A special religious feeling may be called forth by this formula. If used for oneself, it will create a mental temple atmosphere. If this formula is applied to people who have no religious feeling at all, it will cause a certain interest in religion or a sentience for religion. An experienced formula magician may, if he so wishes, instill a religious feeling even into the most stubborn materialist.

A-R

When applying this two-letter key, the formula magician is able to fill his own mind or that of another person with good cheer, to remove melancholic states of depression, and to call forth the ability to solve the most difficult problems.

A-S

If the formula magician wishes to achieve a special understanding of the most profound causes and relevant effects of the electrical fluid, i.e., if he wants to grasp these things intellectually, he will make use of this two-letter key. He may, of course, bring about the same understanding among other people. Using this formula he is furthermore able to awaken the spirit of invention within himself and others, especially when inventions analogous to the electrical fluid are involved.

A-SCH (SH)

In order to be able to immerse oneself penetratingly and thoroughly in any specific matter or object, one should apply the A-SCH formula either to oneself or others, and it will stimulate the intellect to do its work diligently.

A-T

When this letter combination is applied Kabbalistically, it will strengthen the memory for material things in particular. It exerts an especially favorable influence on the mechanical memory, namely when one has to memorize something and retain it. Students and actors and the like would appreciate this formula if only they were able to work Kabbalistically! This two-letter key is also very suitable in cases of retrospective memory regarding material things.

A-U

With the help of this formula, one may comprehend the activities of Divine Providence through one's own intellect. The saying: "God's mill grinds slowly but surely," finds expression in this formula. Every formula magician who seeks, intellectually, to understand the activities of Divine Providence in their total profundity will make use of the A-U formula.

A-W

This formula is particularly helpful in considerably increasing acoustical concentration in the mental body and consciousness of oneself or others. Those who are rather strong emotionally, and who must therefore retain their power of acoustical concentration by force, should make use of this formula. The formula magician who wishes that the words he pronounces in his spirit should be better perceived acoustically over the greatest distance may also apply this formula. It increases one's ability of acoustical concentration, which means that there is a greater condensation of the mental sound waves.

A-Y / A-Ü (UE)

This letter combination imparts greater inspiration in the intellectual sense, especially if one is engaged as a writer or has to do some kind of written work. Naturally, it also imparts the ability to find the right expressions with which to clothe an attribute, virtue, abstract idea, or entire train of thought into words and reduce them to writing. Formula magicians who engage in written work and who work as authors have a great partiality for this formula.

A-Z

This formula is recommended for application, whether for oneself or others, whenever the ability of effortless memorization is desired. In particular, those who wish to attain a phenomenal memory may use it repeatedly. The formula magician may train himself — and, if he so wishes, someone else — to become a genuine mnemonist.

A-Ä (AE)

This letter combination influences the intellectual side regarding physical matter. If, for instance, you wish to attain satisfactory results from the mental plane with regard to physical matter, these may only be achieved with the help of this two-letter combination. The same effect will be brought about with regard to people for whom this key is used.

A-Ö (OE)

The last formula of the A combinations is A-Ö. This two-letter key imparts the ability to solve any problem of Kabbalistic alchemy with effortless ease. The formula magician may use this formula for those of his students who have difficulties in delving into the problems of Kabbalistic alchemy. If one is in doubt about a formula concerning the change of a power or ability, etc. (particularly when experimenting with alchemical transformation based on Kabbalah), or if there are difficulties in applying a letter combination, one should resort to this combination, for it will call forth the desired ability.

I have now described all the letters of the alphabet in their analogous connection to the first letter with regard to the mental effects achieved by them. The intellectual aspect has been particularly stressed since the intellect predominates with the letter A. When more than one letter is used, we speak of a "formula" rather than a "letter." This means that a double letter already represents a Kabbalistic formula in which two powers, analogous to these letters, become effective.

For purely technical reasons, I am unable to go into all the details of every letter. The formula magician has now reached the necessary maturity to appreciate the truth of my repeated assertions that, before he begins the practical study of my third book, he must first have acquired the abilities detailed in the concentration exercises of the three senses as described in my first book, *Initiation into Hermetics*. This will give him a clear picture of the functions of the material, astral and mental bodies, giving him an exact concept of body, soul and spirit as regards himself and others. Without this knowledge, it is impossible to make use of the Kabbalah. Many facts are difficult to convey intellectually, for in Kabbalah especially there exist subtleties that can be grasped only by a practitioner.

The Use of the Two-Letter Key With the Letter B

As indicated when dealing with the single key, B is a letter of polarity in which the electrical and magnetic fluids become effective and which symbolizes the positive and negative principles in the field of virtues and attributes. B therefore incorporates polarity and its use on a Kabbalistic basis. This bipolarity acts positively on the whole alphabetical sequence.

B-A

With the help of this formula (i.e. by its electromagnetic fluid) the intellect is honed and, at the same time, the memory strengthened — their vigor and strength will be increased quantitatively as well as qualitatively. If one works inductively (for oneself), one may differentiate between a bright and a keen intellect. It is difficult to describe the difference between these two concepts in words, but if one considers the fact that thirty-two attributes of the intellect are mentioned in the Hebrew Kabbalah and that a distinction is made between (for example) a bright, a keen, an enlightened intellect, etc., then one will not be surprised to see these differences in the practical work. The same, of course, is true of memory, which in a certain way runs parallel to the intellect and the concept of intellectual abilities.

B-B

With this letter combination, the formula magician increases the ability to create electromagnetic volts for various purposes in the mental plane or mental body, either within himself or in others. In my first book, *Initiation into Hermetics*, I have given a detailed description of the method by which electromagnetic volts are produced. The application of the B-B formula will make it easier to adapt the electromagnetic fluid into the various volt forms.

B-C

The use of this formula makes it possible to impregnate space through Kabbalah, no matter where or to what extent. Each virtue, each attribute that one utters spiritually into a designated area, will be bound to that space, as desired, so that it will work there mentally. The application of the B-C combination depends on the purpose one pursues. The formula magician will under-stand this and know how to apply it correctly.

B-D

The formula magician will make use of this letter combination if he wants to give special strength to his own mental matrix or to that of another. The life cord between the astral and the mental bodies may be strengthened qualitatively as well as quantitatively, particularly the latter, so that (for example) mental patients whose disorder has been caused by a weak mental matrix may be cured by this formula. With this formula, high ranking initiates may, at their discretion, prolong the duration of life between the astral and the mental body if they so desire and if Divine

Providence permits. If the magician, in practicing mental travel, wants to stay outside his astral body for a longer period of time or sojourn in dangerous spheres where negative beings may be visited, he is able to enlarge his mental matrix and strengthen the cord between his mental and astral body with the help of this formula.

B-E

The ability to transfer one's consciousness according to one's wish and to bring about mental effects with the electromagnetic fluid can be easily attained Kabbalistically by applying the B-E formula. In the mental body, this formula brings forth a greater receptivity regarding language in connection with beings, and hence a better understanding of beings whose low intellect makes it difficult for them to express themselves.

B-F

In order to bring about a uniform efficacy of will, intellect and feeling in mental travel or the transfer of consciousness, the application of the B-F formula is recommended. Apart from this, it not only gives one the ability to grasp the efficacy and functioning of the four fundamental attributes of the spirit with reference to the mental, astral and material worlds, but also to influence them at one's discretion with the help of the electromagnetic fluid. One who has not fully comprehended the connections between the will, intellect and feeling, and, as a whole, the so-called "I" consciousness in their relation to the functioning of the electromagnetic fluid may, with this formula, attain the ability to comprehend all these connections. It should be clear from what has been said that the tetrapolar magnet is hereby referred to, with regard to the mental body, the mental matrix and the mental plane.

B-G

When applying this formula, the formula magician will be in a position to remove, from the mental plane, the greatest discord and quarrel and to establish perfect spiritual tranquility. With the help of this formula, the magician attains through his mental body — and as a result of his electromagnetic dynamics — the qualitative and quantitative power to bestow true divine blessings which will not only bring about the relevant effects on the mental, but also on the astral and material, planes.

B-H

Whenever works of divine intuition that must be seen mentally are involved, they can be clearly seen with the help of the B-H formula. In particular, this formula strengthens one's vision and clairvoyance due to its polarity. The formula magician who is not yet able to see visual images clearly will want to apply this formula, because by using this two-letter key repeatedly he will, with regard to his mental sight, attain a very clear view of his visions, i.e., a high resolution of spiritual sight such as physical eyes can never possess. He is able to perceive the most subtle vibrations of the mental kind with his spiritual eyes when he applies this formula. Of course, the formula magician also uses the B-H formula as a means of support for his students who have the necessary maturity but are still unable to perceive the seen vibrations clearly and distinctly. Physical eyesight is also strengthened by this formula if the electromagnetic fluid is focused upon the material eyes.

B-CH

A special gift for languages may be attained by this two-letter key so that one not only gains the mental ability to understand all the languages of humans, animals and beings, but also to recognize whether or not a certain symbol is electromagnetically charged.

Therefore it is possible to assess precisely the effectiveness of the dynamics of a symbol in relation to the electrical fluid and its effects. Kabbalistic initiates are also able, through this formula, to transfer this ability to those who are sufficiently mature.

B-I

With this formula it is possible to remove from one's consciousness any painful memory, unpleasant experience, or any unnecessary pangs of conscience. This two-letter key will be especially appreciated by formula magicians who are oversensitive.

B-J

The formula magician who repeatedly uses this two-letter key is able, by means of the electromagnetic fluid, to disengage the consciousness in every man and being and to bring on a deep state of ecstasy. Ecstatic formulas, however, have nothing to do with hypnotic shock, which is different inasmuch as the will is taken by surprise at the expense of the nervous system. If, however, the B-J formula is uttered in the mental body of some other person, it will put the same into ecstasy at once. This is to say that will, intellect and feeling are emphasized in such a dynamic way that the consciousness cannot keep pace and therefore brings about rapture, but if applied to oneself the formula will bring forth rapture without loss of consciousness.

B-K

Using this letter combination, the formula magician attains the ability to condense the electromagnetic fluid in such a way that it will work actual wonders within the scope of lawfulness. It stands to reason that faith and conviction in the electromagnetic fluid are fortified and strengthened. The student of Kabbalah who has not succeeded in increasing his faith up to the state of manifestation may successfully employ this formula. This ability may also be transferred to other people and is called "transfer of power" or *abhishekha* in the Orient.

B-L

The ability to differentiate moral virtues from the standpoint of the efficacy of the electromagnetic fluid, the plus and the minus, is attainable through the B-L formula. Transferred to someone else, it can influence the plus and minus with regard to the magical equilibrium. The formula magician who wants to initiate his student into the secret of magical equilibrium will influence the student's mental body by means of the B-L formula, by which he may, of course, also achieve a state of perfect harmony within a few moments should he so desire.

B-M

This two-letter key bestows upon the formula magician the ability to mentally master the Water principle perfectly, to bring under his control all the beings and powers that are subject to the Water principle. If the formula magician applies the B-M formula in mental travel, transferring himself into the sphere of the Water spirits, all the Water beings, from the highest to the lowest, will sense his power and be pleased to serve him, without it being necessary for him to assume the shape of a Water being.

B-N

This two-letter key makes it possible for the magician to control any mental matrix, and also to recognize what it contains. This means that he can perceive the mental aura, the emanation of the mental body, and impregnate it at will, whether within himself or others. It goes without saying that he is also able to read the most remote thoughts of a spirit, whether it dwells in a physical or only in an astral body. All beings feel the superior power of such a spiritual, highly developed human being, and will hardly dare to deceive the formula magician deliberately. After using this formula for a longer period of time, one also acquires the ability to read thoughts perfectly and to develop a sharp and penetrating gaze.

B-O

The application of this formula will lead to a perfect harmony in the mental and astral body. The mental vibrations called forth will bring about a state of absolute mental contentment. Furthermore, it will be confirmed to the formula magician that, from the material point of view, success and happiness are the accompanying symptoms of mental contentment.

B-P

This formula changes all pride into deepest humility and reverence and, at the same time, brings on a certain religious feeling. The B-P formula also makes it possible for one to charge any object or picture with the electromagnetic fluid or with a volt created by means of this formula, so that everyone who comes into contact with the charged object or picture will find it beautiful. If this two-letter key is used for material purposes by the mental body, it calls forth the longing for a child and for the love of a child, the reproductive instinct being also kindled thereby.

B-R

If the formula magician wants to acquire a certain ingenuity regarding a mental or astral quality, he may easily achieve this with the B-R formula. After charging the formula with the electromagnetic fluid as a volt, he may also use the formula to influence the freedom of action of any human being at his discretion, and even deprive that man of his will, if he so wishes. However, the formula magician will only do such a thing in the event of an emergency or in the case of mortal danger in order to deprive his enemy of his will or, if need be, of his intellect.

B-S

The ability to become absolute master of the electrical fluid and the gift of prophecy in all fields may be attained by the B-S formula. At the same time, this formula will lead to an excellent aptitude for clairvoyance regarding fate — also viewing the past, present and future. Apart from this, the formula magician will gain complete might over man and animal. With this formula he may, if it seems desirable, instantly call forth a state of hypnosis, or cloud one's consciousness, or bring about sleep — depending upon the way in which he charges the electromagnetic fluid connected with this formula. The B-S formula is of an electrical nature and influences the will, which, if the formula magician so wishes, may be disengaged in any person, thereby causing immediate unconsciousness or hypnotic sleep. Many other phenomena may be brought about with the B-S formula.

B-SCH (SH)

The B-SCH formula may be used to attain the ability of mental ransmutation, i.e. the transformation of one ability into another. It provides the electrical fluid with an especially strong penetrating power — expansion — and particularly enables one to cause many different phenomena in the area where the electrical fluid is to take special effect.

B-T

The ability to master one's own memory or the memory of others may be achieved through the B-T formula. Likewise, Kabbalistic astral magic in all its forms may be expressed by this two-letter key. The formula magician gains absolute might over the elements in all the three worlds — mental, astral and material — with this letter combination.

B-U

This letter combination requires a great sense of responsibility, for it enables the Kabbalist to direct the destiny and karma of any human being and bring it under his control. However, the formula magician will never interfere without careful consideration, since he would be made personally responsible for any inconsiderate action; for the electromagnetic fluid will enter directly into the Akasha when this formula is applied and, from there, will create the relevant situations. Used for oneself, this formula will facilitate the application of the Akasha principle with regard to the various planes. Nor can it be doubted that one may attain the ability to penetrate, with the electromagnetic fluid, into the Akasha principle of physical matter, into our ether.

B-W

With the help of this two-letter key the formula magician may, if he so pleases, enormously increase all medial abilities within himself or other people by means of the electromagnetic fluid. The ability to concentrate — specifically as regards intuitive and sentient concentration or the Water principle — may also be considerably enhanced. In this connection, a higher degree of religious sentience also presents itself. This formula also contributes to better clairaudience and the ability to speak over large distances — acoustic reproduction by way of the electromagnetic fluid over great distances. Furthermore, the formula magician attains complete might over the Water element through the B-W formula and is thereby able to work real wonders in the physical world.

B-Y / B-Ü (UE)

If the formula magician is in need of high inspiration for a certain purpose he will apply the B-Y formula, for by this he will be given the mental ability to unite himself easily with the Akasha principle in all its forms. He can achieve the same with other people if he so desires. Further, there is no doubt that with the help of the B-Y formula the magician is able to determine in advance the fate of any material thing, or direct it according to his own liking respectively.

B-Z

This formula will help one to increase many intellectual abilities within oneself or in other people: above all, a gift and talent for rhetoric, organization, etc. At the same time, the formula magician also attains the ability to forward messages easily over the farthest distances through the air via the Air principle. Apart from this, he is instantly able to paralyze any being, human or animal, with the electromagnetic fluid charged thereby for this purpose. And if he makes use of the inverted letter combination Z-B, he is able to cancel the paralysis.

B-Ä (AE)

This formula will put the magician in a position to consciously influence any wishes, thoughts and actions, as he pleases. With its help he may increase desires and passions, and, vice versa, make them subside at his discretion. Furthermore, he is able to charge the formula so intensely with the help of the electromagnetic fluid that a quicker growth is effected. Magicians who wish to specialize in this work will be enabled to work the Hindu "miracle" of the mango tree quite easily should they wish to do so.

B-Ö (OE)

Using this formula, the magician projects the electromagnetic fluid in the form of light and warmth in order to be able to call forth any phenomena of astral projection. With this two-letter key he is also able to stimulate any kind of healing remedy to bring about a better effect. Since this formula also contains the secret of forming the mental matrix for the production of the philosopher's stone, the magician will be given the ability to stimulate any material object to his own liking.

Thus we conclude the description of the spheres of operation relevant to the application of the B formula category with the entire alphabet. I have mentioned only the most important things, although a wealth of effects may be brought on by the electromagnetic fluid when connected with the relevant formula. If I attempted to detail all of them, they would seem like mere fairy tales to non-initiates, and only the experienced formula magician will regard them as a matter of course.

Now follow the formula combinations with the letter C in their alphabetical sequence, which have a certain relation to transformation, to the Eucharist, to alchemy, to the stimulation of matter and all analogous phases.

The Use of the Two-Letter Key With the Letter C

C-A

By means of the C-A formula one can increase the vitality of all intellectual abilities within oneself and others. When this formula has been mastered, asthmatic ailments of all kinds and bronchial catarrh may be removed. Likewise, all the healing remedies used to cure these diseases may be positively influenced by this two-letter key.

C-B

Any food charged with the C-B formula — in other words, loaded with the electromagnetic volt — increases its nutritional content when supplied to the human body; it will also strengthen the electromagnetic fluid of the material body. Those formula magicians who intend to exert a greater electromagnetic influence in the material world and who wish to engage themselves primarily in the magnetic treatment of diseases will particularly appreciate this two-letter key. Talismans may also be influenced by the C-B formula, provided they have been charged by means of a volt.

C-C

With the application of the C-C formula, mental and astral bodies may be inspired with divine ideas in the following way: the mental body is impregnated by means of meditation and concentration in connection with the C-C formula, and the astral body is impregnated with the specific virtues by means of dynamic breath.

C-D

With the help of this formula, the ability of profound cognition, of penetration into the deep mysteries — expanded "I" consciousness — may be increased in the mental body at will. Likewise, it is possible to increase the perception of love in all its aspects if the formula is brought into connection with dynamic breath. If food is charged with the C-D formula and thus eaten regularly, the semen of a man and the ovum of a woman may be influenced with the virtues which they wish their child to possess. Likewise, the fertility of both man and woman may be influenced most effectively if food and drink or the respective healing remedies are impregnated with this two-letter key.

C-E

The C-E formula helps to increase intuition, especially clairaudience. Also, the ability to dematerialize and materialize beings of all kinds may easily be achieved through this formula.

C-F

This formula contributes to the fortification of harmony in the mental and astral bodies. Positive attributes are fortified and negative ones isolated. If embodied into food as Eucharist, this formula will make the body extremely resistant against any negative influences.

C-G

The C-G formula helps restrain feelings of lust in the mental body, changing them into peace and contentment. In connection with dynamic breath, this formula will make the astral body resist any negative influences, thereby inhibiting the decomposition of elements in the astral body. In the material world, the C-G vibration will bring about wealth or prosperity (depending on Divine Providence and one's karma) if the necessary situations are created in the astral world by the impregnation of an object, preferably a talisman.

C-H

Through this two-letter key, the formula magician may obtain the blessing of Divine Providence and influence his own or someone else's fate at his discretion. If embodied into food and drink, the C-H formula will bring about the realization of all wishes. If clear water is influenced by this formula after four drops of *quinta essentia universalis* — the alchemistic universal tincture — are added to it, the person who drinks the impregnated water will be given any material gift or fulfill any wish that he or she may utter in connection with this formula. At the same time, a rejuvenation or prolongation of life and perfect health may be obtained by embodying or stimulating the C-H formula into the *quinta essentia*. Alchemists who do not know all this usually fail in preparing the *quinta essentia* since they are unable to stimulate it mentally. Not only must the universal tincture be produced materially, it must also be charged and influenced with the analogous connections in an astral and mental manner, apart from other radiations connected to the tetrapolar magnet.

C-CH

The mental rhythm or mental life is brought into harmony with this formula. Applied in the astral in connection with dynamic breath and with intensified concentration exercises of the three senses, this formula brings the astral body into universal rhythm and equips it with all analogous abilities. Likewise, this formula brings about a perfect astral impregnation with regard to vitality, health, resistance, etc. If embodied in food, it can cure all diseases caused by a loss of the magnetic fluid — thus, for example, fever, tuberculosis, cankerous skin diseases, etc.

C-I

The C-I formula is an excellent aid for stimulating all astral functions, which at the same time will be improved and strengthened. In the astral and material worlds it leads to perfect harmony, equilibration, and tranquility. Like many other formulas, this one also contributes to strengthening the power of radiation (emission of the electromagnetic fluid) in the astral and the material body.

C-J

This formula is the so-called formula of sympathy or love and is mostly applied in love magic and sympathetic magic. The mental body is supplied with a wonderful radiation-aura by this letter combination; in the astral body it awakens feelings of sympathy, and in the material body it leads towards unification for procreation and the sexual act. Thus the formula magician connects love magic and the magic of sympathy with this two-letter key. When embodied in food and drink, this formula works as a so-called aphrodisiac which stimulates one's sexual drive. Infertility, sterility and impotence are cured if the relevant remedy is impregnated with this formula.

C-K

This formula removes states of anxiety and depression in the mental body; it cures melancholy, increases one's courage and causes situations in the astral kingdom which bring about wealth and prosperity, depending on one's maturity and karma. When embodied in food, it will produce full-bloodedness and possibly corpulence as well. It is preferred by persons who want to gain weight. Formula magicians who are weak and thin also prefer this formula, for the glandular functions influenced by this letter combination will soon make vigorous human beings out of them. When applied to other people, it will remove mental and psychic disharmonies.

C-L

In the mental kingdom, this formula calls forth a feeling of security; in the astral body it will call forth firmness of character and positive attributes by means of dynamic breath; and it will protect the astral body against the influence of negative attributes, i.e., negative attributes will not arise. At the same time, the astral body will be isolated in such a way that it cannot be attacked by elementaries or elementals. Embodied in food and drink, this formula increases vitality and health, and when food is continuously impregnated with it, one will stop aging.

C-M

In the mental body or the spirit, this formula increases one's sentience and, in the astral body, strengthens the magnetic fluid in a quantitative rather than a qualitative way; the efficacy of the magnetic fluid becomes denser, stronger and more penetrating. When food and drink are impregnated with this formula, personal magnetism and the magnetic material fluid are strengthened and will bring about tranquility and equilibration. The C-M formula is regarded as the principal formula for impregnating the magnetic fluid, whether to charge or condense it. Formula magicians who want to bring about materializations often choose to impregnate themselves with the C-M formula before beginning their work in order to embody a sufficient amount of magnetic fluid. Wherever one deals with a concentration of magnetic fluid, whether in the astral or the material world, this formula is recommended.

C-N

If the formula magician wants to achieve a qualitative or quantitative condensation of the mental matrix, he will apply this formula together with the B-M formula. The astral body will be quantitatively, elementally condensed and made resistant against the disturbing influence of the various unfavorable vibrations which exist in the astral world. With the help of this formula, the gait and movement of any man or animal may be influenced Kabbalistically. Uttered in connection with a condensed magnetic fluid — magnetic dynamics — the C-N formula can bring about the immediate paralysis of a human or an animal (this is especially useful for taming wild animals). Likewise a thief, even one who is far away, may be paralyzed at the location of the theft and kept in that state as long as the formula magician deems it necessary. One is also able to call forth heaviness (gravity) and materiality with this formula. A high ranking magician, however, will never abuse such a formula!

C-O

The C-O formula, too, brings about a perfect harmony of the four fundamental attributes of the spirit, and again normalizes any irregularities that might have been caused by unfavorable situations or destiny. This formula will produce perfect harmony of the electromagnetic fluid and the elements in the human body — astrally, mentally and physically. Embodied in food and drink, the formula may, of course, also be used for turning astral and material bodies into magnets of success and happiness. The formula magician may either achieve this for himself or for anyone else. He will, however, never make his own final decision in such a matter, but leave it up to Divine Providence to inspire him accordingly.

C-P

The C-P formula calls forth excellent sentience in the mental body and absolute psychometry in the astral body; in the physical body it calls forth a strong sexual drive, reproductive instinct, and appeal to the opposite sex, so that he who regularly embodies this formula into food and drink will appeal to and be loved by everyone.

C-R

This formula calls forth a feeling of freedom and independence in the mental body and is preferably used by every formula magician before mental travel. In connection with dynamic breath, it calls forth increased geniality in the astral. The talents that one possesses, and especially the ones that appeal to oneself, are thereby fortified so that one's geniality will never subside. When embodied in food and drink, this formula will develop business acumen in material matters, lead to quick action, bestow resistance, and facilitate the removal of all material hindrances.

C-S

The C-S formula increases one's concentration, particularly one's visual concentration. Connected with dynamic breathing, it will fortify, in the astral body, one's control over humans and animals and will impart the gift of prophecy. If one consumes food and drink impregnated with this formula, the electrical fluid in the human body will be strengthened not only qualitatively but quantitatively, so that any diseases caused by disharmony of the magnetic fluid — for instance: paralysis, rheumatism, muscular atrophy, neurasthenia — will be cured by an invigoration and increase of the electrical fluid.

C-SCH (SH)

This formula calls forth the ability to give the mental body any desired shape at will. In the astral body, on the other hand, it will impart the ability to condense the elements quantitatively in such a manner that they may easily be projected inductively as well as deductively; if the material body is impregnated with this formula, it will be able to resist the might of the elements. If the formula magician wants to specialize in the aforementioned, he will easily be able to make his body so resistant that he may expose himself to any element without being assailed by it. At the same time, the ability to stimulate any matter with the electrical fluid is bestowed upon him with the help of this formula so that he is enabled to work true miracles in the material world.

C-T

Applied in the mental body, this formula imparts an excellent memory; in the astral body it calls forth the possibility of charging any form with virtues and attributes; and in the material body it isolates against any negative influences, from whichever plane they may come. Through this formula, complete protection in any respect may be obtained; hence this letter combination may be regarded as a kind of astral "magic hood" that is irreproachable and unassailable to any spiritual influence.

C-U

To acquire the mental attribute of being a favorite of Divine Providence, the C-U formula is best suited; at the same time, it imparts the might of controlling one's destiny and making strokes of fate easier to bear, i.e., making sure that these do not come in an extreme form all at once, but that they have a gradual and tolerable effect. When applied in the astral body with the help of dynamic breath, this formula will call forth the permanent ability to project the astral body at will, fully conscious and with full power (not only by astral traveling), wherever the magician wants it to go. The formula magician is also able to condense his astral body in the location to which it has been transferred, and even to let it work materially. The formula magician has only to impregnate his food with this formula in order to acquire the necessary assistance for this ability from the material world, too.

C-W

The formula magician will only make use of this formula if he not only wants to develop certain medial abilities but intends to maintain them throughout his life. Furthermore, the C-W formula calls forth a great liking for true mysticism in the mental world; in the astral, it will impart colossal reasoning power and a quick wit. When food and drink are impregnated with this formula, it will be possible to be a master of the magnetic fluid in the material world as well as of the entire Water element — not only of the Water spirits, but the Water element in the material world as well. Helped by the C-W formula in connection with the magnetic fluid, the formula magician, as master of the Water element, may achieve many astonishing things in the treatment of the ailing.

C-Y / C-Ü (UE)

This formula bestows upon the formula magician the mental ability to contact Divine Providence at his discretion. Through this formula, he typically receives the highest intuition and inspiration from Divine Providence, but is in most cases thereafter entrusted with a mission as Its servant. There is no turning back, but also no failing. In the astral, the gift of prophecy and prediction may be attained through this formula. In the material world, the magician is given the ability to change the fate of any thing, whether animal or human, at will. If he also impregnates his food with this formula, he is able to make his physical and astral bodies invisible at his pleasure due to his permanent connection with the Akasha principle. Apart from this, many other things may be achieved with the help of this formula.

C-Z

Helped by this two-letter key, the formula magician may solidify all the abilities of his mental and astral bodies. When eating food impregnated with this formula, one's body will be made tenacious and resistant up until old age. Any disharmony and restlessness will be removed by this formula, and happiness and pleasure will take their place. C-Z is the formula of solidification of everything one wants to achieve in the material world and already possesses in the astral world.

C-Ä (AE)

This formula calls forth contentment in the mental body, complete control over one's own character — i.e., firmness of character — in the astral body, and complete cognition of matter besides its mastery through the tetrapolar magnet in the material world.

C-Ö (OE)

In the mental body, the C-Ö formula allows one to recognize alchemy in all its phases, and allows one to find the true connections to the universal laws. In the astral body, it awakens the ability of continual astral projection, regardless of whether one deals with the projection of universal light, fluids, elements or any other phenomena of transformation. In the material world, this formula, if embodied in food and drink, turns every formula magician into a perfect alchemist who is equipped with all the relevant material knowledge, abilities, etc. This formula is particularly important for those formula magicians who wish someday to become perfect alchemists.

The description of the third letter of the alphabet with regard to its use with the second Kabbalistic key is hereby concluded. Among circles of Hermetic initiates, it is called the second alchemistic key, that is, the alchemistic-Kabbalistic key.

I have had to make my informative descriptions as short as possible. On account of his own experience and knowledge, the magician working with these formulas will, by considering the laws of correspondence, be able to compile many other formula analogies; my statements will help him to achieve this.

The Use of the Two-Letter Key With the Letter D

The description of the D series, which, in combination with each letter of the alphabet, is analogous to all phases of love and eroticism in the mental, astral and material worlds, now follows.

D-A

This letter combination particularly raises and strengthens one's mental consciousness by charging the mental matrix; thus it especially stimulates the intellect. Likewise, one's memory is also strengthened. The formula also serves the purpose of recalling long forgotten reminiscences to mind and of stimulating them. If this formula is applied to an extremely forgetful person, he will develop an excellent memory.

If applied to the astral body, this formula increases one's instinct for self-preservation and one's vitality; it calls forth these attributes very intensively. People who have become weary of life are given new courage and a zest for living. This formula may be very successfully applied to people who are planning suicide: they are suddenly seized by a desire to go on living and are given the courage to face life anew. This formula gives them what is virtually a new life.

When transferred to food and drink, this formula impregnates the male and female semen with various virtues and abilities, if needed and desired. If a woman is pregnant, the fruit of her womb may be impregnated by this formula, i.e., the qualities desired in the child may be embodied in it before its birth. Excellent perception and easy learning may, above all, be inculcated in the child in advance by means of the D-A formula. Other intellectual abilities may, of course, be achieved by this formula as well. If the Kabbalist employs it upon himself in a Eucharistic sense, he will, after frequent and regular use, attain the ability to gain and make use of the knowledge derived from any material objects with regard to Hermetic science and its connections.

D-B

This formula either solidifies or loosens the mental matrix within oneself or in other people, as desired or needed. After frequent use of it with this idea in mind, one attains the ability to call forth any mental body while the person is asleep, no matter how far away it may be, thereby gaining complete control; one is able to give orders to this mental body which will later, immediately after waking up, be positively realized in the spirit of the person concerned. It must, however, be assumed that the Kabbalist will never be misled into giving self-serving or even destructive orders.

When transferred into the astral body, one attains the astral ability to strengthen the electromagnetic fluid in the astral body or to influence it with any idea. Depending on what one intends to do, a strong magnetic power of attraction or repulsion may be called forth by this formula. This is particularly important for the development of sympathy, appeal, etc.

Transferred into the material world, either directly into the material body or by taking in food and drink that has been influenced Eucharistically, this formula will increase magnetic healing power, with the help of which one is even able to work physically. The D-B formula is therefore particularly suitable for magnetopaths who are concerned with the treatment of disease through magnetism. By repeatedly influencing the material body with this formula, an especially strong dynamic of the electromagnetic fluid is achieved. This letter combination is therefore to be used in cases where a strong electromagnetic power is to be applied. This formula is preferred for cases of extreme exhaustion or loss of vital *od*,[4] especially with magnetopaths, for it quickly restores and renews lost energies.

D-C

One makes use of this letter combination when a radical purification of the mental body is to be achieved. Kabbalistic initiates call

---

[4]The term "od" or "odic force" is the vital energy of human beings. For further information please refer to *Initiation Into Hermetics* (Volume I).

this formula "the Kabbalistic mental broom." Wherever a quick purification of thoughts or negative mental attributes is called for — as, for instance, before various magical operations requiring an absolute purity of the spirit — and when absolute harmony and balance are needed for the purpose of mental travel into other spheres, this letter combination may be used with surprising success. When applied repeatedly, this formula brings about increased intuition.

Transferred into the astral body, this formula will purify the same. In short: wherever a sudden equalization of the elements in the astral body is needed, the Kabbalist will apply this letter combination, for, apart from the excellent purification of the elements in the astral body, the astral ability of inspiration is particularly enhanced. There is no doubt that this formula also strengthens the astral matrix.

When applied in a Kabbalistic sense in the material world, this letter combination stimulates any body, whether it is an object, a human body or any other living body. If the formula magician specializes in this combination, he is able to change the electronic vibration that revolves round any body at will, i.e., he may accelerate it or slow it down. Of course, one can also influence and change the qualitative attributes of a body at one's discretion with the help of this formula, especially after having used it for a longer period of time.

One's own power of radiation, or that of someone else's aura, is also increased by applying this formula either directly or Eucharistically, so that it has a dynamic effect which is necessary in various magical operations.

D-D

With the help of this letter combination, and after using it for a substantial period of time, one is able to make the consciousness in one's mental body more subtle, i.e., to refine it so that it becomes receptive to any desirable idea. When transferring this formula to others, one can make the consciousness of a person amenable to any idea that is transferred into his or her mental body. When this formula is applied to the respective person during his or her sleep, his or her consciousness may be made so receptive that any post-hypnotic suggestion can be realized, even one made from a great distance.

Applied to one's own astral body or to that of another person, this formula will enhance and strengthen all erotic aspects in the astral body. It stands to reason that the longing to be loved, the longing for desire and for reconciliation with one's greatest enemy is awakened by this formula.

Transferred into the material world, this letter combination is capable of kindling the elements of any object or substance to their greatest efficacy. The D-D formula is suitable for any work requiring an increased vibration of the elements of the material body in elemental magic. By this formula, the elements are not increased qualitatively but quantitatively.

D-E

Repeated use of this letter combination in the mental body will bring about an excellent gift or talent for intuition and, at the same time, for easily transferring oneself into the consciousness of any person or animal, and of not only knowing everything that takes place in that consciousness but also of placing it under one's control if desired. Initiates prefer to use this letter combination when they want to bestow upon their students an *abhishekha*, i.e., when they intend to carry out a transfer of the power or receptivity of consciousness or the enlightenment of an idea to another person. If, for instance, a student is mature enough, but is not able to understand a problem and deal with it in the right mental way, his guru can enlighten his consciousness with the help of this formula in such a way that the student will comprehend the transferred idea to its full extent. In this way also, various talents and abilities may be transferred mentally.

In the astral world, the magician uses this formula to bridge the distance between himself and his partner, i.e., to clear the way so that his partner will distinctly perceive everything that the Kabbalist utters over great distances. This is called "the Kabbalistic use of clairaudience and of speaking over great distances."

In the material world, this letter formula serves the purpose of condensing an idea in the material world in such a way that it will find material expression. For example: after mastering this formula the Kabbalist is able to condense the universal light in a pitch-dark room so that non-initiates will also be able to see and perceive everything. This letter combination may also be used in connection with space impregnation for the purpose of condensing an idea or an energy in the room itself. It is also excellently suited for charging talismans (whether or not the influence is brought about with fluid condensers), and for charging amulets, pentacles, etc. Transferred Eucharistically in food and drink, this formula will strengthen one's own nerves and the nerves of others. Thus it can be very successfully used for all kinds of nervous diseases.

D-F

This letter combination offers many mental possibilities. Above all, it strengthens the will, increasing both will power and intellect, and it especially enhances empathy in one's consciousness. Therefore this formula is used before mental traveling, for one is then in a position to transfer all reminiscences and experiences gathered in the spheres (or wherever one may have been) into the material world more easily.

When the formula is applied to the astral body or the astral world, any character trait may either be enhanced or inhibited at will, depending on the purpose. The outbreak of negative traits may, above all, be thwarted.

198

In material respects, this letter combination easily removes any disharmony in the body; it helps overcome states of excitement and cures all mental diseases, no matter whether the formula be applied directly or by feeding the material body with Eucharistically influenced food and drink.

D-G

This formula makes it possible to call forth a feeling of reconciliation wherever this is required. Even the most excited mind may be calmed within a few moments. Wherever it is necessary to call forth feelings of reconciliation, friendship, affection, etc., in the mental body, the use of this formula is given preference. This letter combination is also readily applied in love magic, since it calls forth a feeling of blissfulness.

When this combination is directly transferred to the astral world, situations will arise which will lead to good fortune and success in one's enterprises. Wherever domestic disputes, hostility and other astral disharmonies appear, you may apply this formula to change all discord into perfect harmony.

In connection with love magic, situations which will lead to prosperity, good fortune and wealth, etc., may be brought about in the material world by means of this letter combination. If this formula is used in natural magic, greater fertility will be achieved.

D-H

This formula is used to hone one's or another's mental eye so that one can see more clearly and with better penetration in the mental plane. Those Kabbalists who, in their clairvoyant operations, find it difficult to distinguish colors or who do not see clearly enough may distinctly recognize the contours with this letter combination. With regard to somnambulistic mediums, one achieves a clearer and sharper perception by this formula if it is applied during the medium's trance state.

The D-H formula may also be used to rescind any acts of fate. Furthermore, it is applied for sex magic — i.e. volt magic — operations when one uses it to dynamize one's own words and thus attain the astral ability to work suggestively. Wherever one wants success in suggestive work, whether in individual or mass suggestion, this formula may be used. Success will be inevitable. When literary correspondence is dynamized with this letter combination or charged respectively, it can make the receiver carry out all the orders contained therein.

If Eucharistically embodied in food and drink, this formula will help to have any material wish fulfilled by the elements. Many other possibilities for use could be mentioned, but these few hints will be enough to prove the versatility of this formula.

D-CH

When applied mentally, this formula will call forth an excellent gift for language, either within oneself or in other people. With the help of this formula one may inspire any creature, whether spirit, human or animal, with one's own thoughts. Any object may be dynamically impregnated with any idea and stimulated by the application of this formula. The Kabbalist is able to awaken the dead by means of this formula, provided that death has not been caused by severe organic disturbances such as cancer, tuberculosis, etc. On the other hand, people who have died of paralysis of the heart or of an embolism may be called back to life by this formula — but only if no karmic reasons oppose their resurrection and only if the Kabbalist is especially familiar with the use of the cosmic language. With this formula it is possible to bring any aquatic animal under one's control at will, and to coerce any being of the Water element to obey the will of the Kabbalist and to appear visibly at his request.

D-I

The D-I formula, like a number of others, can help to either recall reminiscences and memory images or to delete them at one's pleasure. In material respects, one's memory, especially one's mechanical memory or the ability to memorize may be particularly strengthened by this letter combination. People who must memorize great roles or extensive parts — for instance actors, orators, etc. — will realize that this formula is an aid to their profession. The Kabbalist is also enabled, with the help of the D-I formula, to incite the conscience of a person to greater activity, i.e., to call forth pangs of conscience or to make these subside.

When transferred into the astral world or astral body, the D-I formula will call forth great sympathy and loyalty simultaneously; it is capable of solidifying loyalty that already exists. If this formula is applied to married life and transferred into the astral world, its effects will prevent in advance any disloyalty between husband and wife.

In connection with natural magic, any idea may be easily realized in the material world with this formula. Transferred into food and drink, it will bring success and good fortune in every respect.

D-J

One who makes use of this letter combination may place himself or others into ecstasy — into rapture — at any moment desired. Mediums or people with a medial gift may, with the help of this formula, be put into a somnambulistic state within a few moments.

Transferred into an astral body, this formula calls forth strong sexual instincts in human beings and animals of both sexes.

If this formula is transferred into the material plane of human beings and animals, it will prevent infertility, either by direct use or by embodying it Eucharistically in food and drink.

D-K

This formula enormously increases the power of belief in one's spirit, especially in one's consciousness. The projection of light, or work with universal light, is facilitated if the formula magician repeats this letter combination often.

Applied in the astral, the D-K formula removes any state of anxiety and secures success when courting. It brings about situations in the astral world which will lead to wealth and prosperity.

Materially, this formula may be applied wherever abundant fruit, rich harvests, etc., are expected.

D-L

With this formula it is possible to incorporate into the mental body any desired virtue that is required for one's spirit. It stands to reason that it may also be successfully applied for other people.

Used in the astral, this letter combination subdues any desires or passions, and, apart from this, dissolves any astral elementary.[5]

The D-L formula is especially suitable for prenatal education. As far as health is concerned, food and drink are influenced with the wish that the semen be impregnated with future health. Repeated use of this formula in the material body or by way of the Eucharist will lead to an almost miraculous power of physical resistance and tenacity. A body that has been Kabbalistically impregnated in this manner will be distinguished by its great efficacy in work and sports, and any Kabbalist who wishes to achieve something in competitive sports will make use of this formula.

---

[5] An entity, created by a Magician, consisting of one or more elements. For further details, refer to Step VII of *Initiation Into Hermetics.*

D-M

This letter formula may be successfully applied, either to oneself or others, in order to attain mental brightness and vitality and special interest in mental matters. It transforms mental weariness into mental vigor.

In the astral body, this formula awakens an ardent longing to love and be loved. A volt which, with the help of this formula, is produced and transferred into the astral world to kindle thoughts of love or similar ideas will cause situations that will contribute to the realization of these desires.

In the material world or material body, this letter combination will strengthen the magnetic fluid. The desire for sexual satisfaction is aroused in the opposite sex. If an enforcement of one's own magnetic fluid is required, this letter combination should be used either directly or Eucharistically, i.e., transferred into food and drink. The D-M formula also helps cure any diseases of the Water region (i.e., the abdominal region) in connection with the magnetic fluid. This is particularly true regarding chronic constipation, enterospasm, ascites and all diseases analogous to the Water principle.

D-N

This letter combination reinforces the mental matrix and consequently increases mental receptivity. When applied to oneself or to others, it intensifies the spiritual emanation or aura and enhances the attributes of the spirit. The risk, however, is that when it is applied to other people it may also strengthen the negative qualities of their spirits. Thus one must be very careful when applying this formula to others. If one wants to make use of it for oneself, it is advisable to first repeat the formula that cleanses the mental body.

Applied astrally, this formula will fulfill any desire for love in man and woman. When applied to oneself, it will lead to a blissful wedding, a happy married life and to good and permanent friendships.

In material respects, this letter combination represents an excellent formula for procuring sympathy, calling forth mutual love and attraction.

D-O

By repeating this formula one attains an excellent power or competence of judgment. Whether used for oneself or for others, it will bring about absolute harmony and balance, as well as tranquility of the spirit.

In the astral, situations are caused by this letter combination that will lead to satisfaction in all sorts of love matters.

Embodied in food and drink, this formula may bring about changes in one's tastes so that, for example, bitter coffee may be turned sweet without having to use a sweetening agent. By using this formula, one is even able to change water into wine and vice versa.

D-P

This formula calls forth humility and awe in the spirit. Applied to others, it will bring about the downfall of haughtiness, pride, and conceit, and will give rise to severe pangs of conscience. Even the coldest heart will be melted by the D-P formula.

Astrally, this formula may serve the purpose of stimulating pictures so that they appear to be beautiful and have an appealing effect. By the way, *incubi* and *succubi* may be consciously created with the Kabbalistic use of this formula, for in connection with the strong simulation of a picture there also takes place a strong condensation of it, so that it gives one the impression of being alive and may be persuaded to leave its frame. The stimulation process of the picture may also be perceived by non-initiates.

When applied materially, this formula, like many others of the D series, will also call forth the desire for sexual satisfaction and arouse a longing for children.

D-R

In the mental world or the spirit, this formula brings on a keen mind and awakens the feeling of independence and absolute freedom. It is therefore recommended that this formula be repeated before every mental journey, since it causes an easy separation of the mental body and facilitates mental traveling.

When used in the astral, the D-R formula makes one popular with other people and awakens any kind of geniality that one may wish to possess.

Materially, it imparts extreme skill and manual dexterity and enables one to use one's acquired knowledge in a way that will bear material fruit. Furthermore, this letter combination makes one understand the woes of other people.

D-S

The D-S formula may be used to awaken special enthusiasm, either within oneself or in other people, since it particularly strengthens the electrical fluid in the mental body.

Used astrally, this formula forces people to be obedient and calls forth great submissiveness in the opposite sex. When applied in sex magic, the D-S formula, above all, imparts astral vision into the past, present and future.

In the material world, one may, with the help of this letter combination, cause one's greatest and worst enemy to panic. Moreover, this formula protects against any kind of magical interference, evil influences, etc., intended to hurt or destroy the material body or any other material object.

D-SCH (SH)

In the mental body, this formula will bring about "clair-sophism" ("clair-knowledge"). It is preferred by gurus who want to impart an *abhishekha* — a transfer of consciousness — of particular Hermetic knowledge to their students telepathically. By means of this formula, the ability to comprehend any problem easily is also achieved.

Applied to the astral body, this formula imparts the might of becoming an absolute master of love, one who cannot be intoxicated by any love influences. The formula magician should therefore impregnate his mental body with this formula if he intends to visit the Venus sphere, the sphere of beauty and love, in order to be unaffected by its treacherous charms.

Used materially, any seed may be impregnated in such a magico-Kabbalistic manner as to sprout and grow with supernatural rapidity. In this connection, everyone will certainly remember the well-known "mango tree miracle," which can be realized with this Kabbalistic formula. Any matter may be stimulated and any idea materialized through the D-SCH combination.

D-T

This formula is preferred for strengthening one's own or another's memory. It is also excellently suited for charging talismans with a view to strengthening one's memory.

When applied astrally, it will remove frigidity with regard to the love between a man and a woman, and will enhance the feeling of love in every respect.

In the material body, this formula will strengthen vitality in general; it will help to overcome states of exhaustion, etc. When applied directly or Eucharistically, this letter combination will place the formula magician in a position to impart an extremely strong vitality to the semen and ovum, whether of the male or female, of oneself or another, which will facilitate an easier fertilization provided the genital areas are also Kabbalistically impregnated with this formula.

D-U

This formula particularly calls forth the ability to read another's thoughts, and, further, to know the mental destiny — the past, present and future karma — of oneself or others, and to influence it favorably at will. Every Kabbalist knows that there exists a mental, an astral and a material or physical karma or destiny.

Astrally, this formula combination may be used to influence love affairs. It may also be used to load love talismans.

When applied materially, a telepathic, spiritual bond between man and woman is established and the exchange of feelings made possible. Likewise, this formula strengthens the Akasha principle in the human body, which will be of great advantage for clairvoyance, clairaudience and clairsentience when carried over to physical matter.

D-W

Used as a formula, this letter combination will increase one's concentration, especially with regard to one's sentience, i.e. concentration of feeling. The Kabbalist who is unable to turn his feelings into a dynamic potential, a force field, will find his task easier with the help of this letter combination. Frequent repetition of this formula will awaken various abilities in the mental body.

Applied astrally, this formula produces religious feelings and a mood of holiness, the so-called "temple atmosphere." Furthermore, the D-W formula is also used to impregnate space for the purpose of calling forth such a temple atmosphere, since it awakens a mood of humility and great devotion to the deity being worshipped.

In material respects, this formula ensures the greatest success when courting. That which is unreal can be made believable to the opposite sex; therefore this formula may induce gullibility. It is not used by true initiates except when applied for space impregnation. I have only mentioned it because of its peculiarity.

D-Y / D-Ü (UE)

This letter combination particularly increases the connection to God in the aspect of love. The result is good intuition as well as inspiration in the mental body.

Astrally, this formula imparts a good sentience and allows one to fully comprehend one's love for the opposite sex and, likewise, to fully determine the degree of sentience of love.

This letter combination is regarded as a kind of special formula for charging talismans by means of sex magic. If, for example, this formula is applied to the Akasha principle of a seed, it will not only be possible to influence the latter but to see its mode of operation. If, therefore, the Kabbalist concentrates on the Akasha principle of a seed, applying this formula to it by a transfer of his consciousness, he is enabled not only to see the tree growing from the seed to its full size but also to perceive the entire destiny of the tree.

D-Z

Used Kabbalistically, this formula reinforces all intellectual abilities of the spirit, especially memory, and awakens excellent powers of deduction in the mental body.

After repeated application in the astral, this letter combination will hone any artistic talent and the ability to clothe abstract ideas in words. When concentrated on the head region, this formula will increase one's telepathic receptivity.

If Eucharistically embodied into food and drink, it will lead to tenacity and endurance, and it is especially suitable for great feats in sports. When used for space impregnation, it calls forth great sociability as well as the right mood for entertainment, fun, dancing, etc. Wherever there is a depressing mood in a room, it can be removed by the D-Z formula.

D-Ä (AE)

Like many other formulas of the D series, the D-Ä also awakens thoughts of ardent desire, craving for sexual satisfaction. However, the D-Ä formula may also be successfully applied whenever melancholy and all its side effects are to be removed. This formula brings about situations leading to the satisfaction of personal desires, in particular those relating to love and eroticism.

In material respects, this formula is good against infertility or unfruitfulness and, when applied Eucharistically in food and drink, is good against nightly ejaculations.

D-Ö (OE)

This formula imparts to the mental body the ability to easily master any thought Kabbalistically and to easily change or transmute it into the opposite, if desired. Furthermore, the D-Ö formula also strengthens spiritual perseverance.

Used astrally, this formula subdues any kind of desire or passion, in particular erotic and perverted ones.

In the physical or material world this formula serves to turn one's sexual energies into vitality or any kind of intellectual ability.

The Use of the Two-Letter Key
With the Letter E

All combinations involving the letter E have a secret connection to human consciousness in all three kingdoms, and at the same time to condensation or materialization.

E-A

Used mentally, this formula reinforces one's intuition, expands one's consciousness, facilitates the transfer of consciousness, and hones one's spirit and intellect.

In the astral body, the formula increases one's astral hearing, especially the ability to hear various beings; it enhances might over the air spirits and awakens numerous medial abilities, among them the ability to make proper use of this formula in the astral sense.

Applied materially, this letter combination is capable of calming the greatest storms and tempests. Used Eucharistically, it will cure any asthmatic allergies.

E-B

With this formula, one may impart strong dynamics to any form of ideas as an elemental[6] and thereby facilitate one's work on the mental plane. If repeated before traveling in the mental body, this letter combination imparts a strong resistance which enables one to stay separated from the material body for a longer period of time.

---

[6]An entity created by a Magician on the basis on a conscious thought-form, through his imagination and will power. For further details, refer to Step VI of *Initiation Into Hermetics.*

In the astral body, a stronger charging of the electromagnetic fluid for various purposes is effected by this formula. Likewise, this letter combination also serves for the Kabbalistic charging of talismans, amulets, pentacles, and furthermore for the materialization of beings that are to be transferred to an object by means of electromagnetic volts, and for the Kabbalistic loading of mirrors with fluid condensers, etc.

E-C

The E-C formula may be used to facilitate the conscious comprehension of an abstract idea or concept, and furthermore to incorporate a virtue or ability in the spirit or mental body.

If one wants to sustain an astral ability permanently one also makes use of this letter combination, which is furthermore particularly suitable for the impregnation of astral vigor and balance. This formula is also recommended for use before experiments intended to materialize one's own astral body, whether directly beside one's physical body, or far away from it. This condensation will succeed much more easily.

The E-C formula is used for material purposes, especially if one's physical body is to be rejuvenated. In such a case, food and drink must be impregnated with the E-C formula. After considerable use, one will not only appear to be younger, but one's vigor and vitality will also be increased.

E-D

With the use of this letter combination, it is easy to influence one's subconscious — to awaken, increase, and, in connection with this formula, to make effective in the outside world various intellectual abilities with the help of telepathic suggestion.

Applied astrally, this formula will make one accepted by the opposite sex; its repetition is therefore recommended before any kind of courting or when attempting to gain the favor of other personalities. When applied to oneself, the E-D formula endows one with the power of attraction and makes one very sympathetic in the eyes of other people.

Regarding the material world, a seed may be brought to sprout more quickly with the help of this letter combination; fertility in nature may be promoted, one's sexual energy may be influenced favorably, and success may be brought about in any situation, especially with regard to friendship, etc. One who uses this formula Eucharistically — who impregnates food and drink with it and eats and drinks it thus — will turn from a thin man into a corpulent one.

E-E

Applied in the mental body as a Kabbalistic formula, this combination will facilitate the mental travel of that body. The transfer of one's consciousness, either to a certain place or into a certain object, can also be achieved with this formula. If it is applied to those who suffer from disturbances of the consciousness, they will recover their normal consciousness. The E-E combination is also regarded as a protective formula against inebriation; he who makes use of it cannot become intoxicated or suffer any disorder of consciousness. If it is Kabbalistically cast into the astral body of a drunken man, he will become sober at once.

Applied to one's own astral body, this formula calls forth astral hearing. If it is used in connection with the impregnation of a room, everyone in that room will easily perceive the invisible world, beings, etc., without difficulty. When impregnating a room over a great distance, the Kabbalist, helped by this formula, is able to utter his words in such a way that they will be heard by magically untrained people who are present in that room — be the distance ever so great — with as much clarity as if the Kabbalist were there himself. However, it is recommended that such an impregnation of a room be dissolved at once after use, for otherwise all kinds of mischievous spirits and elementaries are likely to haunt it, and these beings may then also be perceived by the untrained.

In the material world, a favorable ability of projection is attained by this formula, and the fluid condensers may be charged with it for the purpose of carrying out the materialization of a being, elemental, elementary, etc. Anything that is to become more physical is easily materialized with the help of this formula.

E-F

Absolute mental equilibrium, as well as absolute spiritual tranquility and equilibrium, may be achieved with this letter combination. If applied to married couples who are constantly quarreling, they will soon be reconciled. The greatest rage will be turned into serenity and peace. This formula may therefore be used wherever mollification is required. Even the most agitated mind may be calmed within a few moments.

Applied astrally, a quick purification of one's astral aura — which will then shine like a wonderful light — is achieved with this letter combination. This formula can awaken a feeling of peace and security in others, and make them experience a well-balanced sense of blissfulness.

In the mental world, this formula will increase the vitality of the human body. Magnetopaths are fond of making use of this formula when they want to reinforce their own vitality Kabbalistically. The E-F formula is capable of rapidly renewing lost vitality, or reinforcing weakened magnetism. This formula will exert a universal influence on physical health, especially with regard to nervous diseases. If transferred to food and drink, it strengthens the individual elements of the food, thus stimulating it to become more effective. Concentrated in healing remedies or fluid condensers, this formula will particularly increase the healing or healing effect.

E-G

This formula removes absent-mindedness, imparts inner peace, enables one to bear karmic vicissitudes more easily, and leads to the realization that, from the Hermetic point of view, everything happens justly, whether it seems right or wrong in our opinion; everything that happens has its reason. To arrive at this understanding is to have the blessing of Divine Providence, which can be achieved either for oneself or for others with the help of this formula.

When used astrally, this formula bestows inspiration as to how happiness and success may be achieved. A volt that has been formed and charged for the astral plane by means of this letter combination will cause situations that will bring about good fortune and success and everything one wishes to achieve (unless it is karmically inadmissible) and will initiate everything necessary to attain one's final goal. This formula is especially suitable for people who are really unlucky. After repeated use, it will lead to absolute contentment.

When used in the physical body and the material world, this formula will protect against any kind of material losses, lead to wealth and prosperity, and increase these gradually. Embodied in food and drink, this formula is a proven remedy for anemia and chlorosis, since it quickly forms red blood cells and favorably influences glandular activity and blood circulation.

E-H

If there is a problem of particular importance which needs direct inspiration from Divine Providence, it is recommended that the problem be transferred into the Akasha or causal principle by repeating the E-H formula several times, and then entering the negative state, i.e., vacancy of mind. The first inspiration is always the right one and may therefore be regarded as the answer. If, apart from this, the formula is mentally uttered into both eyes and likewise repeated, it is capable of honing the mental eye — or, Hermetically speaking, of spiritually cleansing the eyes — so that one gets a clearer mental picture. This formula is therefore particularly suitable for clairvoyants who must make daily use of their spiritual vision. The repeated use of the mental eye weakens one's physical eyesight; the use of this letter combination is recommended in order to avoid this.

In the astral body, the E-H formula makes one invulnerable to astral influences; the astral body is almost mummified by this formula so that it becomes practically unassailable. Furthermore, this letter combination protects against decomposition through astral elements, and makes the astral body resistant so that the good and noble attributes may never be shaken. The astral body is thus spared any temptation and will anticipate in advance any approaching danger.

With regard to the material body, the E-H formula causes the situations the Kabbalist wishes for. Applied to other persons, this formula makes a success of all undertakings and fulfills any material wishes. Transferred Eucharistically into food and drink, it makes the physical body resistant to any kind of disease.

E-CH

In the mental kingdom or mental body, this formula leads to clair-sophism or clair-knowledge and develops the ability to read the intentions of any human consciousness and to transfer one's own consciousness into any spirit, man or animal, or to identify oneself completely with any object. In other words, an absolute control of the consciousness of spiritual beings, humans and animals is achieved with the help of this letter formula. At the same time, the use of this formula imparts a gift for psychometry.

When this formula is mastered in the astral body, one attains a gift for clairaudience over short and long distances, into both the past and the present. The rhythm of life in all its phases, in nature and in man, may also be influenced with this formula, which means that when this formula is mastered it is also possible to awaken the dead by restoring the rhythm to their hearts (providing that their physical bodies have not suffered from a severe disease which has already deteriorated the person during their lifetime). Likewise, people who are hard of hearing but who have no anatomical defect may be released from their complaint by using the E-CH formula if it is rhythmically applied to their ears.

In material respects, many Kabbalistic feats may be carried out by means of the E-CH formula together with the Water element. Thus, for instance, water may be kept fresh constantly; it may be made to evaporate momentarily in front of the eyes of onlookers; it may be brought forth in the driest desert or, if required, even directly from a rock. In the magic of nature, rain may be caused through this formula, fog may be called forth, and water may be made solid (this does not refer to its transformation into ice). Many other phenomena, which will sound unbelievable to the non-initiate, may be called forth by the true application of the E-CH formula.

E-I

Only experienced Kabbalists should make use of this formula, for with its help it is possible to transfer the spirit back into previous incarnations whereby the reminiscences of former lives on earth, with all their knowledge and experiences, may be released to the full consciousness of the Kabbalist. If the Kabbalist allows this to happen, he becomes fully responsible for his former incarnations and their fate, which will then be transferred to his present life. In most cases, this curiosity is paid for dearly. I only mention this formula, firstly, to point out its peculiarity and the dangers involved and, secondly, not to cause a gap in the series of the letter E. Bearing the indicated dangers in mind, the Kabbalist will only make use of this formula in cases of emergency. If, however, the Kabbalist is able to offer Divine Providence an appropriate reason for his exploration of the past — for instance, to explore the karma of others — he may use this letter combination safely.

By using this formula in the astral, all the astral functions, regardless of which type they may be, are increased and stimulated to more intensive activity. The E-I formula stimulates the activity of the elements in the astral body — but with the disadvantage that, due to the great effectiveness of the formula, the negative effects of the elements are also unfortunately increased, and then have to be inhibited by means of other suitable letter formulas. The E-I formula reinforces the instinct for self-preservation and may therefore also be applied to people who have become weary of life.

If the E-I formula is mastered in the material world, too, one's muscular strength may be doubled or tripled by its help. After repeated use, and especially if transferred to food and drink, this formula makes one attain enormous muscular strength, even when one's physical body may appear to be much weaker. The feats of strength achieved with the help of this formula border on to the miraculous: thus thick iron bars may be bent, heavy stones lifted, and many other things.

E-J

Mentally, a medium may be placed simultaneously into a state of trance and a state of ecstasy by this formula. It delivers the spirit from the bonds of the astral body, and the medium is enabled to look across time and space and relay truthfully, to the Kabbalist, that which is seen. Applied to oneself, this formula facilitates an easy exteriorization of the mental and the astral body. Likewise, it allows all impressions and experiences to be taken over into normal consciousness, in particular all those things that were perceived through speech.

This formula may be very successfully applied in mummial[7] sympathetic magic. Likewise, clairaudience is easily attained by mummial magic in connection with this formula. The practice is as follows: two partners of an equal state of development prepare two similar mummies or wax figures, influencing them with their own blood. Then they enliven them with the help of this formula. If one operator speaks into a mummy at the pre-arranged time, the other operator, after having placed the other mummy to his ear, will clearly hear every word that is spoken, irrespective of the distance. Then the roles are changed; the transmitter becomes receiver, and vice versa. This is called mummial telegraphy. Both wax figures must, of course, be charged with the E-J formula in order to guarantee success. I only mention this practice because of its peculiarity.

If, in the material world, this formula is transferred into the sexual sphere, it will excite and stimulate sexual intercourse. This formula may also be used to increase one's sexual energy. Furthermore, it will enhance the fertility of a woman and serve as an aphrodisiac for both men and women.

E-K

Applied mentally, this formula will especially strengthen the power opposed to the Fire element and the will, and therefore reinforce the state of manifestation of one's belief. The formula contributes to the realization of everything one believes in and wishes to possess within the shortest time, due to one's knowledge of the universal laws and a belief in the laws of analogy. In general, absolute certainty is obtained by this formula, together with a strong belief in everything in which one is interested and

---

[7]Any part of one's body, such as hair, skin, bodily fluids, and so on.

which one wants to have realized; and the elements will fulfill these wishes automatically without having to cause situations for their realization first. If the formula is used for other people, it will guarantee them absolute certainty in their undertakings.

In the astral, this formula will bring about absolute tranquility, decisiveness and perspicacity, so that one will be able to resist even the greatest dangers and never lose one's astral equilibrium. Hostile people will keep out of the way of an astral body that has been influenced by this letter combination, because they feel its superiority. If this formula is applied to others, it will awaken resolution, courage and perseverance in them.

If transferred to food and drink, this formula increases the electromagnetic energy, especially if used for material purposes. Volts that are formed for achieving prosperity should be charged with this letter combination.

E-L

This formula combination will endow the spirit with the ability to easily look through the character and virtues of any human being and to analyze them without difficulty, and, furthermore, to read the thoughts of other people. When applied to oneself, this formula awakens an excellent ability for analytical combinations which will be especially advantageous to writers.

When used for oneself astrally, this formula will bring about firmness of character, and mental tranquility so great that it will never be shaken by anything. Applied to the astral bodies of other people, this letter combination awakens trust, so that these people will confess to the Kabbalist their good as well as their bad deeds. It will make the most taciturn man talkative and compliant. If the region of the neck is influenced by this formula, the result will be an especially great perseverance in talking — a result which is particularly appreciated by those who are required to do a great deal of speaking in their profession. Helped by this formula, they will not easily become tired of speaking.

This formula makes one's physical body healthier and more resistant, and endows it with stronger nervous energy and greater vitality. Therefore this formula may be used for all kinds of nervous diseases. Unless they have an organic defect, mute persons who have lost their ability of speech due to a shock can regain it.

E-M

In the mental body, this formula will increase clairsentient and psychometric abilities — but other medial abilities that are analogous to sentience may also be awakened and reinforced by this formula. With the correct Kabbalistic use of this letter combination, even the most insensible man may be instilled with the feelings one wishes him to have; the most unscrupulous criminal will have thoughts of repentance and pangs of conscience through this formula.

When this combination is used in the astral, one may easily call forth beings of the Water element and make them speak and sing; the singing of the water naiads is extremely beautiful. Apart from this, the ability to differentiate astral tone vibrations properly and to use them for various purposes may be obtained with the help of the E-M formula; one may thereby learn astral sound magic.

Embodied materially into food and drink, the E-M formula increases the magnetic fluid. This formula is used wherever an extremely strong magnetic energy is required for an experiment, whether for healing or for any other kind of magnetic magic. If the formula is used skillfully, fish may easily be paralyzed in the water so that one can catch them with one's bare hands. When this formula is banished into a volt, one's greatest enemy may, in case of great danger to one's life, be momentarily transfixed; even the most dangerous animal will be unable to move.

E-N

This formula is used in connection with the "mental protective coat." If, by using this formula, one surrounds oneself with a mental wall, known as an *odic* protective coat, one cannot be penetrated or influenced by any power, whether positive or negative, for this is a state of perfect mental insulation.

In the astral, this formula protects any room, building, etc. It not only offers protection against bad influences, but also against elementary occurrences like lightning, etc. Furthermore, if a room is impregnated with this formula accordingly, it guards against thieves; no being, whether spiritual or material, is then able to enter the impregnated room, and if it should dare to do so it will panic and leave the place at once. The E-N formula thus secures perfect protection against any assault and any influence. As long as the room remains impregnated, neither a good nor an evil being is able to enter the room in question.

In material respects, everything that moves — be it a man, an animal, or even an invisible being — can be paralyzed instantaneously with this formula, so that he or it will not be able to move from the spot. If this influence is to be dissolved again, the formula must be repeated in reverse, as N-E. Also, volts serving various purposes may be formed with the help of this formula, which is generally used in that way in order to attract things. This formula makes heavy objects light and light objects heavy. Many more Kabbalistic tasks analogous to the ones stated here may be carried out in connection with this formula.

E-O

Used mentally, this formula can force the greatest liar to tell the truth, the worst criminal to admit his foul deeds, and any member of the opposite sex to confess infidelity. If this formula is applied to a person during sleep, that person will admit everything he or she has done, without being aware of the confession. If the E-O formula is used for oneself, it enables one to attain excellent powers of judgment. The desire to make amends for any indiscretion is thereby awakened, as is an uncompromising sense of honesty.

Applied astrally, this formula awakens an inclination to asceticism and spiritual independence. If applied astrally to others, it will lead to absolute contentment and good fortune in all undertakings. The inspiration necessary for success, the required impulse and suggestion, will always come at the right moment.

If applied materially to one's enemies, it will initiate the process of karmic reprisal. Used for oneself repeatedly, whether Eucharistically or directly, this formula will bring about outstanding success in all undertakings as well as good luck at games.

E-P

This combination calls forth a strong religious feeling in the spirit or mental body, joined with the deepest humility. The Kabbalist typically uses this formula before prayer, profound meditation, or work in the Akasha in order to awaken the right mood and to enhance his intuitive talents. For insensitive human beings or persons who have absolutely no regard for any religious sentience, the use of this formula is recommended to awaken such feelings within them.

If this formula is used in the astral, it will call forth the equilibrium of the elements. Therefore, it pays well to use it for temptations which are difficult to overcome — for instance, overcoming the charms of the opposite sex, etc. Apart from this, the formula should be repeated before mental travel to the Venus sphere, in order to be protected against the negative elements there and so that their intended influences and allurements fail to work. Likewise, when traveling to other spheres — for instance, to the sphere of Mars — the E-P formula offers great advantages, for one will never condemn the negative, but will be strengthened in the conviction that everything happens with good reason and must therefore come to pass. The Kabbalist will consequently assume the same attitude towards all spheric beings, i.e., he will remain neutral and never condemn anything.

Applied materially — whether via food and drink or directly to the material plane — this formula will awaken a strong reproductive drive and a longing to have children and their love. This letter combination enables one to Kabbalistically impregnate and influence his semen before sexual intercourse in such a way that only the semen particle under that influence will cause conception, and will generate a child of the sex the Kabbalist has chosen.

E-R

In the spirit or mental body, this formula combination especially strengthens the intellect and releases a feeling of independence and absolute freedom of the will. Mentally, for example, this formula may be used to form and charge volts for the purpose of freeing someone from prison, particularly if that person has been wrongly convicted. The use of this formula also proves itself in law suits where the truth is to be revealed and absolute justice must be done.

Used in the astral, this formula calls forth fabulous geniality and increases one's inspiration. Apart from this, many other positive talents may be awakened in the astral body by means of this formula.

Materially, this letter combination will secure outstanding success in many different fields of knowledge. With the help of this formula, whoever is engaged with literature will have his literary work met by the approval of a great circle of readers.

E-S

In the mental body, this formula reinforces the electrical fluid and the will power and, apart from this, expands one's consciousness.

The E-S formula may be used to master the electrical fluid in such a way that its effect may even be transferred to a single point, for it enables one to acquire such or similar abilities. The E-S formula also contributes to an increase in one's intellectual activities, i.e., to the development of great perseverance. Furthermore, one's clairvoyance — especially prophetic clairvoyance — may also be increased by this formula, whether visions into the past, present or future, or visions over time and space. Likewise, one attains the ability to transfer one's own thoughts and wishes to an animal.

When applying this formula to the material body, one can bring about instantaneous hypnosis or deep sleep. Furthermore, there is no doubt that the consciousness of any human being may be influenced and mastered at one's discretion with the use of this formula. When it is embodied in food and drink for oneself, insomnia may easily be cured. The effect of sleeping remedies may likewise be increased if they are charged with the E-S formula.

E-SCH (SH)

If this combination is mentally applied to oneself, it considerably strengthens the power of one's belief, mastering the light with all its variations and possibilities. It calls forth the highest enlightenment and is especially suitable for solving difficult problems which require brilliant solutions. This formula is a universal remedy for enlightening the intellect. Since the E-SCH formula also increases the power of belief, as mentioned above, it is possible to have every word uttered in the spirit or any wish expressed through the formula realized in all three kingdoms by means of the corresponding elements, if desired.

When the formula is applied materially, it is possible to condense power, whether in the whole body or in certain parts of it, in such a way that the parts of the body are no longer subject to a single element. Thus invulnerability, incombustibility and unassailability may be achieved. The E-SCH formula also imparts the ability to master the electrical fluid and its condensation in the material world fully, in order to carry out operations of transmutation in a Kabbalistic way. Wherever an especially strong fluid is required, the application of this formula is recommended. This formula should also be employed in the treatment of various diseases which require the reinforcement of the electrical fluid. If the formula magician intends to bring about Kabbalistic phenomena — for instance, lighting a candle with concentrated electrical fluid or influencing a thunderstorm, i.e., lightning and thunder — or forming especially strong electrical volts for such purposes, he will prefer to make use of this formula combination.

E-T

Used mentally, this formula is capable of increasing one's intuitive memory in an exceptional manner; it gives new life to long forgotten ideas.

Applied astrally, the formula strengthens one's might over the elements, and with its help it is possible to dynamize, in a Kabbalistic manner, various elementaries and elementals so strongly that the use of universal light or elemental matter is not necessary at all. Therefore this formula is preferred in any operation of astral magic where the reinforcement or dynamization of a power is concerned.

When transferred to food and drink, this formula helps to prolong life and remove physical disharmonies; it thus strengthens health and the astral bond between body and soul. Great resistance is achieved thereby, enabling all sorts of useful applications in practical life where special physical endurance is required.

E-U

The mental application of this formula facilitates an easy transfer into the Akasha principle, i.e., the achievement, regardless of what is intended thereby, of a state of trance, whether clairvoyance, clairaudience, clairsentience, or the calling forth of positive effects in a direct manner — for example, changing a destiny, producing volts and transferring them into the Akasha principle, and so on. By frequent repetition of this formula, one's intuition is greatly increased.

When the formula is successfully applied to the astral body, it may easily be separated, whether from one's own or someone else's body, since the transfer of this formula into the astral matrix effects an easy separation of the same, thus facilitating the projection of the astral body.

If food and drink are influenced by this formula and then consumed, the ability of materialization on the material plane will be increased. This letter combination may be successfully used for materialization media and for the condensation of spiritual beings. In connection with space impregnations, spiritual beings will appear which can easily be seen and felt, possibly even by people who have not been spiritually trained. Connected with the loading of fluid condensers or with mirror-magic, this formula facilitates the actual viewing of the materialized picture. Wherever something condensable is involved — whether thoughts, astral or mental forms, beings, etc. — this formula may be applied with outstanding success.

E-W

When this formula is applied to oneself in the mental plane it will call forth increased medial abilities, especially clairsentience and psychometry. When raising the concentration of feelings, this formula may also be used with good success. Persons who are very analytical, who possess a dominating intellect which lacks intuition and sentience, may readily make use of this formula, for it will awaken a greater receptivity of sentience when used repeatedly. Of course, it may also be applied to people who are said to be insensitive in general.

After frequent repetition in the astral, this letter combination will develop one's clairvoyance and the ability to speak over great distances.

Applied materially, this formula helps one to easily overcome any obstacle, so that the Kabbalist who influences food and drink with this formula will overcome grievances, sorrows and pains more easily, thus becoming well balanced. The magnetic fluid in the physical body is particularly strengthened. If magnetopaths use this formula, they are able to successfully treat all diseases analogous to the Fire element and the electrical fluid — thus, for example, inflammations, fevers, etc., where a strong magnetic fluid is present. Many other things can be favorably influenced with this letter combination: for instance, operations of natural magic, the charging of talismans, and so on.

E-Y / E-Ü (UE)

This formula combination facilitates a strong connection with God. Furthermore, it awakens a strong feeling of cosmic love. If it is often repeated in the mental body, it will call forth all the mental abilities that arise from cosmic love. The Kabbalist is able to impregnate his own spirit with this formula in such a manner that even the greatest enemy will be unable to do him any harm.

As regards astral abilities, this formula has an influence on the gift of prophecy or the mantic ability regarding destiny in the material world. If this formula is skillfully applied as a sort of "magical hood," it will make the Kabbalist invisible and he will not be noticed on his mental travels. Thus it contributes excellently to mental and astral invisibility, so that a medium or clairvoyant who is not trained in the Kabbalah will be unable to see a mental or astral body influenced with the help of this formula, either in the mental or in the astral world. It stands to reason that the invisibility attained by this formula is also maintained during mental travel to other spheres.

This type of invisibility may also be transferred to the physical body. However, longer training is required until one is able to condense the formula in such a way that it becomes capable of really changing the electronic vibrations or the aura of man — thus, for instance, the formula may be loaded into a volt. Furthermore, the Kabbalist is enabled, with the help of this formula, to erase a photographic picture that has been taken either on a film plate or a roll of film. If the Kabbalist does not wish to be photographed, or if this is done against his will or without his knowledge, he is able to erase the negative, causing the plate or film to become black. Many other possibilities could be mentioned, but one who genuinely understands the laws of analogy will be able to find them for himself.

E-Z

After repeated use, this formula will impart an excellent power of judgment, a special quickness or repartee, and good powers of deduction as well as the ability to penetrate deeply into any particular subject.

Used astrally, this combination will bring forth artistic talents, especially oratorical and literary ones. The formula may also be used to reinforce within oneself the ability to "send messages through the air," i.e., to bridge time and space and to clairaudiently perceive, over great distances, everything that is spoken. Furthermore, the formula is of great use when connecting oneself with the relevant object so that the things said in the astral at great distances may be simultaneously perceived through clairaudience.

If food and drink are influenced by this letter combination, great endurance in athletic feats will be effected by a thorough strengthening of the nervous system. When used as an aid in space impregnations, the E-Z formula cheers one's feelings and favorably influences everything that is analogous to a happy character, as, for instance, enthusiasm for singing, dancing and other entertainments. Wherever depression prevails, this formula can bring about the opposite.

E-Ä (AE)

The most secret thoughts and wishes of the mental body concerning the material world may be realized with the help of the E-Ä formula. Through inspiration and intuition, the Kabbalist is shown ways and means to fulfill his desires. If the Kabbalist repeats the E-Ä formula often, he will have access to inspirational warnings should he make any false step.

By using this formula, any material wish uttered in connection with elemental magic can also be realized at once. Everything the Kabbalist wishes to quickly realize materially and, vice versa, everything he wants to remove from the world, will be achieved with the help of this formula.

E-Ö (OE)

If the Kabbalist uses the E-Ö formula, he will gain the ability to perceive, understand and master the whole sequence of a subject matter, even if he has only been able to learn part of it. If, for instance, he is aware of only one of a man's mental abilities, he is able to ascertain, with the E-Ö formula, all the other mental attributes which that man possesses, one by one. If the Kabbalist thinks it necessary, he may also master those abilities so that the man in question will appear to him quite exposed — like the image in a mirror — without being able to hide anything from him.

If the Kabbalist applies this formula in the astral, he is also capable of condensing his orders over great distances in such a way that they will strike like thunder. Everything that produces sound, whether astrally or materially, may be condensed, reinforced and projected by means of this letter combination. This formula is therefore rightly called the astral tone of all sound vibrations, tone vibrations, and also of all color and emotional vibrations.

This is only a minor example of the numerous important functions of this formula. The Kabbalist will no doubt work out further variations for himself. If he is able to use this formula well, he is in a position to influence and master the astral vibration of any body, even of speeding up or slowing down the vibrations of electrons in order to cause any desired modification of the quality of an object. This formula is therefore called the "qualitative transmutation formula."

If I were to deal with all the formulas of the two-letter key in all its combinations, I would have to describe 27 x 27 = 729 letter combinations. However, the two-letter key being a rather difficult one, I have detailed only the first five letters of the alphabet as examples thereof, assuming that the advanced and experienced Kabbalist will understand, on account of the laws of analogy, how to work with all the other letters of the alphabet properly, and assuming that he will compile, at his discretion, further formulas regarding the two-letter key if, in his opinion, the examples given by me do not suffice.

It should be considered that the following key, the three-letter key, has 27 x 27 x 27 = 19,683 letter combinations and the four-letter key 531,441 letter combinations, i.e., 27 raised to the fourth power. To describe all of them is manifestly impossible.

In this book I describe a number of formulas analogous to each key. However, my work is not to be regarded as a Kabbalistic dictionary; instead, it contains concrete explanations of the four Kabbalistic keys.

With regard to the two-letter key, I am now going to indicate to the Kabbalist, as a further aid, the mental attributes of the letter series.

Then I shall inform him concerning the attributes of the three-letter and four-letter keys by way of one-letter formulae, the so-called "basic key" through which all the other letter combinations may be compiled.

Taking the letters of the alphabet in sequence and applying them mentally in regards to the two-letter key, everything referring to the letter:

A — is analogous to the enlightened intellect, the ability of judgment, comprehension of the profoundest truths, knowledge and ability of perception, and the unfolding of all intellectual abilities. To the letter:

B — all the letter combinations which impart absolute power over the electromagnetic fluid in all spheres are correspondent. This is the mastery over polarity. To the letter:

C — the influences of all divine ideas, virtues and attributes are subject. To the letter:

D — everything connected to consciousness and the mental matrix are correspondences. Furthermore, D expands the "I" consciousness everywhere and leads to wisdom. To the letter:

E — everything related to the transfer of consciousness and intuition is a correspondence. To the letter:

F — everything that refers to the unification of the basic attributes of the spirit — everything connected with the will, intellect and feeling as "I" consciousness. To the letter:

G — everything analogous to divine blessing — for instance, mercy, peace, forgiveness, etc. To the letter:

H — everything that is meant by intuition regarding Divine Providence. To the letter:

CH — everything having an analogous connection to linguistic talent, whether the languages of beings, humans or animals, or the understanding of symbols. To the letter:

I — everything relating to conscience, remembering and memory. To the letter:

J — everything connected with ecstasy and rapture. To the letter:

K — everything concerning the state of manifestation of belief. To the letter:

L — everything regarding the spiritual comprehension of true morality from the Hermetic point of view. To the letter:

M — everything referring to feeling, life and sentience. To the letter:

N — everything concerning the mental aura and the mental matrix with regard to the aura. To the letter:

O — everything analogous to the fundamental attributes of the spirit with regard to harmony, destiny and lawfulness. To the letter:

P — everything that has to do with religious sentience and deepest humility. To the letter:

R — everything concerning freedom of will, freedom of action and intellectuality. To the letter:

S — everything regarding enthusiasm and the absolute control of the electrical fluid. To the letter:

SCH — everything connected to the highest enlightenment, spiritualization, and the rapture related to these (i.e., enlightened intellect). To the letter:

T — all aspects of influence over the memory. To the letter:

U — everything relating to the ability to work in the Akasha principle, in all forms of existence, likewise the highest intuition, karma, or the mastering of one's destiny. To the letter:

W — everything pertaining to clairsentience and psychometry, as well as all other medial abilities. To the letter:

Y(Ü) — everything having to do with inspiration in connection with intuition, through the connection to God and love, and the mental abilities arising therefrom. To the letter:

Z — everything which brings about the raising of general intellectual abilities and which has special influence on memory. To the letter:

Ä — the realization of wishes regarding physical matter. To the letter:

Ö — anything of a mental nature which requires transformation.

All the letters may be brought into harmony with the meanings indicated here and the desired formulas composed. By using the examples given here, the Kabbalist is offered a vast selection of combinations or formulas.

The two-letter key is the most important one in regards to the spirit and the mental plane when applied to the astral and the material worlds, with all its wishes and the like.

It is unnecessary to indicate all the formulas one after the other. Depending on one's purpose and intention, the aforementioned letter combinations may suffice for the practicing formula magician. In any case, he will be able to compose further letter combinations for specific purposes by making use of the letters of the alphabet and their correspondences to mental qualities. If desired, the astrological analogies may also be called upon; likewise, the Kabbalist may avail himself of the keys of the elements — the elemental correspondences of the letters and their analogous connections to color and sound — and compose, on his own, further analogous formulas with the two-letter key, or even the three-letter and four-letter keys. Never will he make a mistake in so doing!

Step IX
The Use of the
Three-Letter Key

With the three-letter key, the Kabbalist will work Kabbalistically either directly on the astral body or the astral plane. The formula magician and Kabbalist knows that all situations which come to pass in the material world as destiny or external effects are created in the astral world by the elements in connection with the electromagnetic fluid which comes forth from out of the elements. Therefore, the astral world is the world of situations.

*   The application of the three-letter key or astral key to the astral world is effected by transferring the first letter of each triple-letter formula into the mental world.

*   The second letter of the triple-letter formula is Kabbalistically transferred into the astral world.

*   The third and last letter of the triple-letter formula, being the letter of realization, is either volted, Eucharistically transferred into food and drink, or brought into connection with the breath, either inductively or deductively — and it stands to reason that it is not the normal inhalation of air, but the imagination and the inductive and deductive application of the concentration exercises of the three senses connected with the letter as inhalation and exhalation, that is meant by this.

The analogous connections are to be seen indicatively from the letters. However, apart from these I shall mention such analogies of the alphabetic series of letters as are not well-known and which require a really profound intuition. By so doing, I hope to facilitate somewhat the Kabbalist's exploration of further operational spheres of the three-letter key.

The practicing Kabbalist will regard this as a matter of course, but it will be difficult for the theorist to find analogous connections.

A

Astrally, the letter A corresponds to the acquisition of all the talents that are analogous to the Air principle — music, oratory, acting, etc. Among occult abilities, the following fall within this astral category: "far hearing," clairaudience, levitation, power over the Air element in the astral kingdom, and all the correspondences pertaining to Air. Also, the language of symbols may be connected with this letter to a certain extent.

B

imparts the ability to form magical volts, charge talismans, know and master the mysteries of sex magic, and attain astral intuitions.

C

offers everything relating to the impregnation of the astral body with virtues, attributes, etc.

D

is analogous to eroticism in all its aspects.

E

has reference to everything relating to clairaudience and inspiration, including inspiration through the spoken word (i.e., the inner voice).

F

has reference to all the correspondences relating to the tetrapolar magnet in the astral world, taking into consideration the elements and the person's character traits.

G

is related to everything that contributes to contentment, blissfulness, prosperity, good fortune, success, etc., and has reference to everything leading to these situations.

H

imparts the ability to influence one's destiny or karma with Kabbalistic formulas. Everything connected with Kabbalah, the comprehension of this high science in all its aspects and analogies, is subject, in the astral, to the sphere of influence of this letter.

CH

influences everything relating to the mystery of rhythm and life and the power to master these.

I

has reference to the astral matrix with all its functions.

J

influences everything that has to do with sympathy and antipathy, including mummial magic, love magic, love magic involving entities, etc.

K

brings into harmony everything that corresponds to courage, endurance and decisiveness.

L

has reference to everything relating to the astral equilibrium in respect to one's character and psychic spiritualization.

M

influences all effects and analogies relating to the pure magnetic fluid or the pure astral Water element.

N

influences everything pertaining to the instinct of self-preservation and, furthermore, everything that binds the astral body to the zone girdling the earth, i.e., the astral body's astral-magnetic powers of attraction to the zone girdling the earth, with all its analogies and possibilities of application.

O

influences everything that creates situations leading to perfect contentment, in every respect whatsoever.

P

is analogous to everything connected to the yearning to ennoble one's character and to the perception of beauty.

R

All dispositions of astral nature that can be brought together with astral geniality are subject to this letter.

S

Everything regarding clairvoyance, the gift of prophecy as well as power over humans and animals, is analogous to the astral lawfulness of this letter.

SCH (SH)

is related to the manifestation of one's belief with all its analogous connections. At the same time, all the letters which possess the power of transmutation are subject to this letter. This letter imparts the disposition to achieve control over all the elements in the astral kingdom, and especially over the electrical fluid and the Fire principle.

T

is analogous to all astral magic practices in all their forms, especially those which lead to power over the elements.

U

Everything connected with projection of the astral body, with the arbitrary transfer of consciousness, with states of trance, and with the ability to call forth these talents, etc., is analogous to the letter U.

W

The gift for long-distance hearing and speaking comes under the occult astral analogy of this letter, as does everything connected with the predilection for true mysticism and religion.

Y / Ü (UE)

influences everything in connection with the gift of prophecy with regard to destiny and physical matter.

Z

Everything related to artistic ability — whatever art may be involved — is subject to this letter. The astral ability to "send messages through the air", or of astral telepathy corresponding to the Akasha principle bridging time and space, has an analogous connection to this letter.

Ä (AE)

corresponds to everything analogous to desires, passions, self-satisfaction, whether one is concerned with controlling them or calling them forth.

Ö (OE)

corresponds to all astral projections and all forms deriving therefrom.

Using the above-mentioned analogies in connection with the letters of the two-letter and one-letter key as indicated in this book, the Kabbalist will be able to compose as many formulas as he may desire. He may build up as many as 19,683 formulas of the most varied subtleties and modes of action. It stands to reason that he does not really need all these combinations; in most cases, he will be content with a few and will be able to do ample work with these.

Because of their peculiarity, I am now going to indicate some formulas of the three-letter key which I did not discover by universal analogy but which were confided to me by a very high spiritual being. Only a truly experienced Kabbalist of the highest rank will be in a position to ascertain the analogous connections.

Thus the formula S-A-L points to the three powers which are effective in the three worlds — mental, astral and material — by the merciful influence of Divine Providence. These three powers make it possible for the Kabbalist to become absolute master over all three kingdoms on account of Universal Divine Love.

E-R-J is another formula of the three-letter key which enables the Kabbalist to recognize the seventy attributes in all seven spheres in his consciousness. The seventy fundamental attributes are the seventy stages that are effective in the seven spheres, and by their Kabbalistic use the various powers and abilities may be achieved.

The formula M-J-H imparts the astral ability to penetrate into the most secret analogies of divine names and their letters. The M-J-H formula, entrusted to the biblical Moses by the same high being who confided it to the author, enabled him to experience the most profound Kabbalistic knowledge. On account of his cognition, he was able to use it practically in order to work all his wonders.

H-CH-S, used Kabbalistically as a formula, enables the magician to achieve the highest wisdom.

E-M-N imparts the ability to know and master the divine name analogous to the seventy powers in the universe. This formula, however, has nothing to do with the formation of the 72-letter name, since E-M-N is a secret formula entrusted only to a few high initiates by high spiritual beings of the sphere of Jupiter.

With the formula N-N-A the three-dimensional blessing — mental, astral and material — of Divine Providence is bestowed upon the Kabbalist.

The formula N-J-T bestows upon the Kabbalist the ability to recognize absolute truth in every respect through Divine Providence.

N-M-M is the Kabbalistic secret relating to the strength and might of silence with all its analogous connections.

J-L-J signifies the comprehension and reception of the highest light of the Divinity and — like God the Creator — the possession of the manifestation state of belief, i.e., the highest aspect of Divine Omnipotence.

H-R-CH is a divine Kabbalistic formula which is used for the glorification of Divine Providence in various rituals.

M-C-R is the divine manifestation of the Akasha principle in all three kingdoms. Through the Kabbalistic use of this formula one attains the ability to do creative work in all three kingdoms simultaneously.

The formula W-M-B gives one the power necessary to call upon all the spheres with their intelligences and to direct their attention upon oneself. This formula, however, should only be used at a moment of greatest danger.

If one wants to bring about cosmic effects through universal love, one may use the formula J-H-H, by which everything analogous to love that the Kabbalist wishes may be realized.

M-CH-J is a formula of worship of the Akasha principle in all three worlds.

The formula D-M-B, when used Kabbalistically, makes all seven basic powers of the spheres unite as a single power and enables the Kabbalist to achieve anything he wishes.

CH-B-W is a secret name for Divine Providence with its four aspects. This formula is used for all kinds of Kabbalistic evocations and venerations in order to obtain, by supplication, things normally unattainable.

By means of the formula R-A-H, all the principals of the ten spheres may be called upon all at once and their help enlisted. However, the Kabbalist should seldom make use of this formula; he will incur too great a responsibility, and an abuse would be greatly disadvantageous to him. The most experienced Kabbalist will, of course, know this formula, but will not make use of it without good reason.

With the help of the E-L-M formula, the omnipotence of working creatively in all spheres will be attained. The Kabbalist will only apply this formula if he has been directed by Divine Providence to carry out a mission that makes these Kabbalistic powers necessary.

The same applies to the M-H-SCH formula, which enables one to work the greatest miracles that are at all possible.

By means of the A-K-A formula, the experienced Kabbalist is able to raise the dead.

The formula L-A-W calms storms at sea. If the Kabbalist uses this formula, he will be able to work all kinds of water miracles, for instance walking on water, etc. Moses was able to divide the Red Sea with the help of this formula so that he and his people could cross it without getting their feet wet and without danger.

Moses was entrusted with another formula — the M-B-H formula — which also enabled him to work miracles.

With the H-R-J formula, Divine Providence may be called upon in all Its aspects and in all kingdoms and spheres, and may also be honored. He who Kabbalistically utters a request with this formula will always be heard by Divine Providence. However, he must be sure that his request is lawfully justified.

With the F-H-L formula, divine universal love is called upon and everything attainable by the aspect of Divine Love may thus be achieved.

The M-L-H formula is also a divine universal formula of love which will make the formula magician acquainted with the working of Divine Love in all its aspects, and will place him in the state of the highest blissfulness of Divine Love.

With the CH-H-Ve formula, Divine Providence is called upon, which controls the four elements. The Kabbalist who applies this formula Kabbalistically — mentally, astrally and materially or Eucharistically — becomes absolute master over the four elements in all three kingdoms.

The formula J-CH-W expresses the absolute might of God. The Kabbalist who makes use of this formula receives the same absolute might as is possessed by the Creator. It is not to be feared that the experienced Kabbalist working with this formula will ever abuse it, and if an impure and immature human being whose intentions were not in harmony with the universal laws ever ventured to make use of it he would face the absolute annihilation of his personality. One must therefore proceed very cautiously!

The M-N-D formula endowed Moses and all the prophets of the highest schools of prophecy with absolute knowledge and enlightened intellect. Furthermore, it gave them permission to bequeath the highest knowledge — although only through symbols — to the material world. It was this formula which enlightened Moses when he formulated the Ten Commandments.

With the formula H-H-H one is given the ability to impart energy to any letter so that it will become Kabbalistically effective even in the Akasha principle.

With the J-Z-H formula, divine mercy in its highest aspects is called upon; it is used wherever lawfulness, justice, etc., no longer suffice. J-Z-H is a very high Kabbalistic formula.

It would be difficult to establish, through the universal key, the analogous connections of all these formulas, for they are a secret and can only be conveyed traditionally or entrusted to a Kabbalist by a being of the highest rank. I was also entrusted with formulas that are very dangerous; to prevent any abuse, I refrain from publishing them. Whoever has achieved maturity and is entrusted with a divine mission may learn many more secrets regarding the formulas. I do not have permission to write about all of the secrets, for they do not all correspond to the third Tarot card, but refer to further arcana. The formulas indicated here are published merely because of their peculiarity. Mere theoretical knowledge will not suffice for genuine use, and anyone trying to use these formulas without the appropriate preparation will only be greatly disappointed. He who attempts to make use of these formulas with evil and selfish intentions in mind exposes himself to the punishment of Divine Providence, the details of which I do not wish to mention here. He would be guilty of what the Bible calls "a sin against the spirit."

In Kabbalistic writings, the Divine Name JHWH is frequently mentioned and described. I will now indicate some Kabbalistic influences of these 3-4 letters, i.e., of the Jod-He-Vau-He, and what may be achieved by them in the mental and astral as well as the material world.

By the three-letter name JHW, in which the second H is missing, the Kabbalistic ability of miraculous healing may be attained. If the letters are three-dimensionally volted by Kabbalah, this formula may be used for protection against assaults by enemies. Should anyone dare to attack the Kabbalist in spite of this, the protective volts produced in the astral, mental and material worlds can bring about the death of the assailant. The JHW formula is therefore called the Kabbalistic formula of backlash.

Furthermore, the three letter-name JHW may also be used in connection with another letter which is not to be regarded as a formula but merely used phonetically as a basic letter. If, for instance, the J is connected with an o, the latter must be regarded as a small letter following the former. Only the J is used, i.e., volted, Kabbalistically, but is phonetically pronounced Jo. The same principle applies to the second, third and fourth letters. The formula Jo-Ho-W, used Kabbalistically in the mental, astral and material worlds, leads to the absolute might of achieving everything in all these realms.

The formula Ja-Ha-W creates — via the mental and astral world, and thence into the material world — all the situations that lead to wealth and prosperity in the material world.

The formula Jö-Hö-W brings about perfect harmony in the mental, astral and material worlds if used mentally, astrally and materially (Eucharistically) — which then must result in perfect health.

The same formula, when connected with o rather than ö, (i.e., Jo-Ho-W) leads to absolute might as possessed by Omnipotence, which also means absolute mastery over health, be it one's own, that of other human beings, or that of animals.

The gift for prophecy, whether mental, astral or material, may be attained Kabbalistically by the two formulas Ju-H-W and We-He-Bi.

Love and friendship, for oneself as well as for others, may be achieved by the JHW formula, i.e., by Je-He-W.

To attain joy one should use the formula Jo-Ho-W; the same may be achieved with Wo-Ho-W.

Success in matters of friendship is brought about with the formula Ji-Wi-H, and also with Ju-H-W, Ja-H-W, Ji-H-W, and with the pure J-H-W.

All these formula combinations can also bring about the annihilation of an enemy. This is not to say that the Kabbalist himself becomes the attacker; rather, the enemy destroys himself with these Kabbalistic formulas. The Kabbalist who masters them attains the highest degree of protection.

Special protection against negative beings of all kinds and from all spheres is offered by the formula Ju-H-W.

Particular good fortune in all undertakings is secured with the help of the Kabbalistic Jau-H-W formula. Contentment is brought about by Je-W-W.

These are only a few hints as to the practical use of formulas based on the three-letter name JHW. There are many others; some of these, however, are of a secret nature and may not be discussed — neither do they belong within the scope of the third Tarot card.

The formula A-L-Z offers absolute control over the Air principle as well as control over Air spirits of all ranks.

The O-W-Y formula imparts mastery over the spirits of the Earth. So does the formula G-O-B.

With these few examples I now conclude my treatise on the use of the three-letter key and the use of divine names through three-letter formulas. All these formulas are traditional and, since time immemorial, have always been entrusted by very high-ranking intelligences to only a few initiates. They have been kept strictly secret up until this point. Since this is a matter pertaining to the third Tarot card, the description of which has been permitted by Divine Providence, I have been allowed to publish a few formulas.

Footnote to the three-letter key:

The Kabbalist will surely notice that the Tattvic Table of Correspondences is but a small fraction of the knowledge of the elements, and that in Hindu terminology the elements have names consisting of three letters. I indicate these names as a footnote; their respective correspondences will be found in the relevant literature.

The LAM formula is analogous to the Earth principle.
The VAM formula is analogous to the Water principle.
The PAM formula is analogous to the Air principle.
The RAM formula is analogous to the Fire principle.
The HAM formula is analogous to the Akasha principle.

This terminology will lead every reader to the universal mantra of AUM, which represents the so-called Brahma formula.

Step X
The Use of the Four-Letter Key

In Step IX, I gave a detailed description of the three-letter key and its use. I shall now pass on to the last key, the four-letter key, which I am also allowed to make public. This key represents the whole mystery of the Jod-He-Vau-He, the so-called Tetragrammatonic key or key of realization. It is the secret of the magic square or the tetrapolar magnet. From the numerological point of view, the number 4 is analogous to Jupiter and represents lawfulness or justice. There are several ways of applying the four-letter key. I shall indicate the most important ones.

In the case of the four-letter key, one works with four basic letters which have to be applied in the Kabbalistic manner. The most common use of the four-letter key is the application of a four-letter formula or combination of four letters (no matter which one) in the following manner:

The first letter is Kabbalistically transferred into the Akasha principle, the second letter into the mental world or — if necessary and depending on what the Kabbalist intends to do — into the mental body, the third letter into the astral world, and the fourth letter into the material world, either directly or Eucharistically.

The second mode of use is to transfer two letters into the Akasha and two into the mental world or mental body. In this case, one letter is intended for the respective plane and the other one for the respective spirit or body.

If, for example, one wishes to attain a mental ability which may be realized by the four-letter key, then the first letter is transferred into the Akasha principle and the next one into the mental body. These two letters then work directly on the mental body from the Akasha principle, just like the two-letter key. The third letter is also transferred into the Akasha principle and, from there, influences the mental plane. The fourth letter is transferred directly into the mental world.

This is the highest form by which two letters from the Akasha principle may exercise their influence on the spirit and on the mental or spiritual plane simultaneously. This is the so-called bipolar application of the four-letter key.

The next method of application is to transfer two letters (which are always the first two letters) into the mental world by Kabbalah — that is, one of them into the mental body and the other into the mental plane. Of the remaining letters, the third is transferred into the astral body and the fourth into the astral world; and in this manner they become effective.

Another use of the four-letter key is to transfer two letters each into the astral world and, at the same time, into the astral body: this is called direct astral Kabbalism. The astral body is thereby influenced bipolarly by two letters, while the other two letters are transferred into the astral world to create the preconditions and situations necessary for the realization of the respective wish.

In yet another application, two letters are transferred into the astral world to create the situations necessary for the realization of the respective wish, while the remaining two letters either influence the material body directly or are divided in such a way that the third letter is transferred into the body by Kabbalistic letter impregnation of the whole body and the fourth exercises its influence in a Eucharistic manner through food and drink.

Thus there are many possible variations; the question of which one to use should be decided in accordance with what one wants to achieve. All keys, regardless of the manner in which they are applied, will bring about their full effect; for in this case one works creatively with the Divine Name or tetrapolar magnet, the absolute lawfulness of God. Whether one's wishes concern the astral, mental or material world, the realization is achieved by those elements that pertain to the respective letters together with the electric, magnetic or electromagnetic fluid analogous to them.

If, however, one wishes to have something realized from the causal principle directly into the material world without a particular reason, it is recommended to begin with the method indicated first by transferring:

* the first letter into the Akasha principle;
* the second into the mental world or the mental body when dealing with wishes that concern the Kabbalist himself;
* the third letter into the astral body; and
* the fourth, Eucharistically, into the material world.

If, however, someone else's wishes are to be realized, this mode of application of the four-letter key — which refers to the mental, astral and material body — should not be chosen, but the four-letter key should be applied in the following manner whenever wishes for success, good fortune and other events of destiny are in question:

* the first letter is transferred into the Akasha principle;
* the second one into the mental world;
* the third one into the astral world; and
* the fourth one as a volt into the material world.

The way in which a letter may be used Kabbalistically has already been indicated in the description of the one-letter key. Referring to this key once more, I may point out that the Kabbalist accepts full responsibility when working directly from the Akasha principle, whether he employs one letter or two, for in so doing nothing is entered into the Book of Destiny and only

Divine Providence in Its highest form alone will decide on success or failure.

When using the one-letter key, the Kabbalist is the creator who himself carries out the act of creation in accordance with the universal laws and, therefore, is fully responsible for his action. The danger is very great in this case, and therefore the Kabbalist should always consider well whether he can actually accept the responsibility for that which he undertakes Kabbalistically.

It may be rightly assumed that the practicing Kabbalist and formula magician who has already achieved such a moral and ethical development will not be the cause of anything irresponsible or unlawful. But still, my warning is justified; when choosing the Kabbalistic key, the Kabbalist should be very cautious and consider things well.

If the Kabbalist works with the four-letter key in all the other spheres without transferring at least one letter into the Akasha principle, he causes karma — depending, however, on the plane in which he is working and for which he is using the letter combination. He must be aware of the fact that mental causes bring on a mental karma or destiny, astral causes an astral karma, and material causes a material karma, therefore releasing material effects.

I have described but a few modes of application. If the Kabbalist knows all the letter analogies well, he also knows how to work, how to apply this or that analogy, and into which sphere he should transfer it. He is given a free hand in the choice of the key.

The four-letter key is no doubt the most effective one, for it is the key of realization wherever the Kabbalist himself works creatively without the elements being able to resist him or any force oppose him. The four-letter key makes the formula magician an absolute master, one who resembles the Creator; for by means of the four-letter key, the Jod-He-Vau-He, the tetrapolar magnet, the Creator has created everything that exists in all kingdoms and planes of our planet.

According to the letter analogies there are 531,441 formulas or formula combinations altogether which result from the four-letter key and its combinations; it is impossible to describe all of them in this book. Therefore, it is left up to the magician to compose formulas which are appropriate to the four-letter key in the manner which I have described in reference to the one-letter key and in accordance with the analogies of the mental and astral world as regards the two-letter and three-letter keys.

To make things easier for the reader, I shall give him, as I have done with the preceding keys, a series of letter meanings regarding the material world which may be of some use to him in composing further letter combinations. The analogies to the material world are as follows:

Letter:

A — secures absolute might over the material Air principle in the material world; thus, for instance, mastery over the Air spirits, control over storms, and the treatment of diseases analogous to the Air principle, such as chest ailments, etc.

B — leads one to become absolute master over the electro-magnetic fluid in the material world and, furthermore, to redress any disharmony in the human body or the physical world, to cure any disease, to become master over life and death in the material world, and to control all four kingdoms — mineral, vegetable, animal and human.

C — offers the ability to control the enlivening processes of physical matter, or, in Kabbalistic terms, to become a perfect alchemist.

D — controls the analogy of all seeds, semens and sperms in the material sense and in the vegetable, animal and human kingdoms, regarding fertility and procreation.

251

E — conceals the secret of materialization and dematerialization of all forms of existence and all possibilities in the material world, whether one is dealing with the materialization of beings, forms of ideas, or whatever.

F — is analogous to the secret of the quadrature of the circle, to the tetrapolar magnet, both in the material world and with respect to the human body.

G — corresponds to everything that has to do with increase, riches and prosperity in the material world.

H — influences the "Let it be!" in the material world, which is to say that this letter will realize any material wish.

CH — stands for absolute mastery over the Water element and the magnetic fluid in the material world.

I — controls all laws of analogy between the micro- and macrocosm and has complete control over measure, number and weight.

J — is analogous to everything that is propagated in the material world; with respect to humankind, it has an analogous connection to the sexual act.

K — like G, is influential with respect to wealth and prosperity in the material world.

L — corresponds to physical vitality, to perfect health and physical harmony.

M — is analogous to everything fluid and controls the fluid state in the micro- and macrocosm, and thus also the magnetic fluid and the attractive force in the material world.

N — Everything in connection with the movement and gait of man and animal is analogous to this letter. So, too, is the force that keeps everything together, the cohesive force of physical matter, and likewise the attractive force, the gravity, of all material things.

O — is analogous to the electromagnetic fluid in the human body, but also influences higher spheres when used in astrophysics. At the same time, this letter produces good fortune and success in the material world with regard to all undertakings.

P — Everything in the material world that is connected to the reproductive instinct in vegetables, animals and human beings is analogous to the letter P. Qualitatively, this letter is expressed in the material world by a love for children and, with respect to the animal kingdom, for the welfare of the young ones.

R — Everything related to intellectual knowledge and rational cognition and experience is connected to this letter.

S — Everything connected with the control of one's consciousness in the material world, be it sleep, hypnosis, anesthesia, or other invasions of consciousness, is analogous to this letter.

SCH — is analogous to the electrical fluid and the material element of Fire and has a great physical stimulating ability. This letter may prevent a physical body of whatever type from being attacked by the Fire element, therefore making it invulnerable.

T — corresponds to the laws of analogy of all three kingdoms and controls the knowledge thereof as well as their practical application.

U — is, like the letter F, analogous to the tetrapolar magnet regarding all physical matter, whether it relates to its penetration or control.

W — Everything in the material world that is somehow connected with the transitoriness of things, whether by delusion, deception, etc., has an analogous connection to the letter W. It also controls the magnetic fluid and the Water element.

Y(Ü) — has an analogous connection to the workings of the Akasha principle in the material world and the physical body. Since it corresponds to the Akasha principle in the material world, it can, when used with the appropriate letter combination, also cause invisibility in the material world.

Z — Everything that is somehow connected with the Air principle in our material world is represented by the letter Z. When applying it Kabbalistically, one is in a position to call forth storms or to abate them, and to influence anything that is related to the Air principle. Applied to the human body, it brings about endurance and tenacity. It is, in general, analogous to cheerfulness and joy, to dancing and similar entertainment.

Ä — represents physical matter in the material world.

Ö — the last letter of our alphabet, controls material processes of enlivening and, from the alchemical point of view, has a direct connection with the philosopher's stone.

This information on the correspondences of each letter with regard to their significance in the material world will no doubt be a useful aid for the formula magician in his correct application of the four-letter key. It will now depend on his discretion, his work, and his intuition as to which formulas he will personally compose should the ones indicated in this book not suffice.

Formulas of the Elements

These offer various possibilities for use. One formula, for instance, is for obtaining might over each element; another one is for might over the magnetic fluids, or qualitative power over the elements; and yet another application of a formula of the elements gives power over the beings that are in the elements:

regarding the Fire element, over the salamanders;
regarding the Air element, over the sylphs;
regarding the Water element, over the nymphs; and
regarding the Earth element, over the gnomes.

Apart from this, a formula of the elements may be used for condensing the primordial principle of an element in different spheres, as is done in the case of volt loadings. A formula of the elements may also be useful for the materialization of elemental beings. A formula of the elements also serves the purpose of acquiring perfect control over the qualitative forms of the elements, or of appropriating to oneself certain qualitative attributes of the elements; and furthermore of carrying out — qualitatively and quantitatively — mental, astral or material impregnations, including space impregnations. Finally, the use of an element formula is suitable for working with element magic.

I will now give a few examples which may serve as a guideline to the experienced Kabbalist who wishes to compose, on his own, the letter combinations necessary for a formula in accordance with the universal key of analogies.

Analogies to the Fire Element

in the Akasha	—	SCH
in the mental kingdom	—	H
in the astral kingdom	—	S
in physical matter	—	T

Analogies to the Air Element

in the Akasha	—	A
in the mental kingdom	—	C
in the astral kingdom	—	L
in physical matter	—	H

Note that the Fire principle in the mental kingdom and the Air principle in physical matter have one and the same letter, expressing the activity of the Air principle in the material world.

Analogies to the Water Element

in the Akasha	—	M
in the mental kingdom	—	N
in the astral kingdom	—	W
in physical matter	—	G

Analogies to the Earth Element

in the Akasha	—	Ä (AE)
in the mental kingdom	—	I
in the astral kingdom	—	F
in physical matter	—	R

This tabulation results in a chart which I reproduce below for easy reference:

Element	Fire	Air	Water	Earth
Akasha	SCH	A	M	Ä
Mental	H	C	N	I
Astral	S	L	W	F
Matter	T	H	G	R

To attain absolute mastery over the Fire principle, i.e., might over the Fire element in the Akasha principle, in the mental, astral and material worlds, the series of letters of the four-letter key is to be applied in the following way:

SCH is Kabbalistically transferred into the Akasha,

H   into the mental body,

S   into the astral body, and

T   into the material world.

The formula for the four-letter key thus being: SCH-H-S-T.

If one wants to attain mastery over the electrical fluid in all three kingdoms, the SCH and the H are Kabbalistically transferred into the Akasha principle and the S and T into the mental body.

If one wants to evoke salamanders by means of these four letters, or achieve mastery over all Fire spirits regardless of their rank, the letters SCH and H are transferred into the mental body and the mental kingdom; S and T, on the other hand, are transferred into the astral body and the astral kingdom.

For example, when impregnating a space for the purpose of causing Fire beings to make a visible appearance, the letters SCH and H have to be transferred astrally into the room impregnation in a Kabbalistic manner, while the letters S and T must be uttered aloud, materially, in a Kabbalistic manner.

If the formula magician intends to use the Fire element for a certain purpose in the material plane, he must utter the letters SCH and H Kabbalistically into the astral world and form two volts out of the S and the T; the T takes the inner part and the S the outer form. In so doing, the T formula has to be brought into harmony with heat and the S with light. Look at the following diagram:

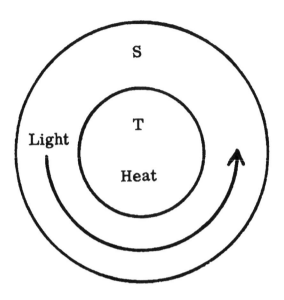

This demonstrative example shows the Kabbalist how the Fire element may be used Kabbalistically for all kinds of operations and magical work. The same system applies to the Air principle, if one wants to master that principle in all three kingdoms:

A-in the Akasha,
C-in the mental body,
L-in the astral body, and
H-in the material world (Eucharistically in the material body).

Absolute mastery over the Water principle is achieved by following the same system and procedure with the aid of the formula M-N-W-G, and mastery over the Earth principle in the same way with the formula Ä-I-F-R.

Referring to the chart indicated, it should be noted that the formula combinations in the horizontal rows are to be used when mastery over all the elements — in the Akasha principle as well as in the mental, astral and, if necessary, in the material planes — is the issue:

directly from the Akasha principle by the formula SCH-A-M-Ä;
in the mental body, i.e., for mental mastery over all the elements, by the formula H-C-N-I;
astrally by S-L-W-F; and
materially (Eucharistically) by the formula T-H-G-R.

The last four-letter formula mentioned indicates the material mastery of the elements, which is usually brought about by the Eucharist, by embodying one letter after another in food and drink.

Having given these explanations indicating the possible variations, I may now conclude this chapter on the use of the four-letter key in respect to formulas of the elements.

Just as the three-letter key J-H-W denotes the name of God, so the four-letter key, the formula J-H-W-H, serves the same purpose.

This four-letter name of God is very often called Jehovah or Adonai in the Hebrew Kabbalah.

As a matter of interest, I may at least indicate a few combinations of the four-letter key with the letters J-H-W-H. If I were to mention all the keys that are Kabbalistically analogous to this name, I should have to indicate 256 formulas, which is impossible for technical reasons. Thus I have chosen such formulas as are, firstly, less known, and, secondly, used only by Kabbalists who are well acquainted with the Hebrew Kabbalah.

The pure formula J-H-W-H, without any phonetic annex of other letters, is generally used for curing severely ill people by Kabbalah. Depending on the way in which this formula is charged or the purpose it should serve, it may also be successfully used for business matters.

If the first letter of this formula is given a phonetic annex in the form of another letter, many more things may be achieved by it. Thus, for instance, the formula Ja-H-W-H brings wealth and success in love, and is also effectively used for curing the mentally ill.

The formula Je-H-W-H helps one to attain the friendship of very important persons, awakens love, and leads especially to erotic satisfaction.

The formula Ji-H-W-H imparts power over friends and makes it possible to learn about their future.

The formula Jo-H-W-H helps one gain control over other people and also imparts superiority over other beings.

The formula Ju-H-W-H secures the acquisition of astrological knowledge, makes one see the connections between the planets of our universe, and leads to power on our earth. One can also make use of this formula for the purpose of gaining divine mercy.

A very effective formula combination with a phonetic annex is Jau-H-W-H, which brings about and contributes to happy moods, realizes plans for the future, leads to wealth, and so on.

Finally, I would like to direct the reader's attention to Jou-H-W-H, which gives protection against negative spiritual beings and leads to good fortune.

When working with these formula combinations of the four-letter key, the Kabbalist will transfer the letter J into the Akasha, whereas the letters that have no phonetic annex are applied by the same analogy to the mental and astral worlds and to the physical.

If the Kabbalist wants to make use of the same formulas by applying the general key, he need only use:

the mental effects	—	into the H
the astral effects	—	into the W
and the material effects	—	into the second H.

For correct Kabbalistic practice, it is very important to know all these things. Depending on the situation and the desire, the Kabbalist will have this or that key at his disposal and will make use of it at his discretion. As already mentioned, the four-letter key is the key of realization and thus one of the most important keys of our planet, since it is analogous to universal lawfulness.

I have not been given permission to specify any further keys. The Kabbalist who strives honestly will be entrusted by Divine Providence with the secrets of all the other keys, one after the other, depending on his state of maturity. These four keys will be quite sufficient for him to understand and apply the cosmic language and the creative words.

I may repeat once again that without sufficient preparation and mastery of the concentration exercises of the three senses, no one will be able to work Kabbalistically or creatively or to penetrate into the mysteries of the cosmic language, to say nothing of its practical use. Mere knowledge of the Kabbalah and its keys is of no avail if one lacks the necessary preparation.

Thus, if the reader should think that he will be able to work miracles simply through theoretical knowledge and the mere perusal of this book, he will be greatly mistaken. Should he try, despite it all, to apply any formula practically without being sufficiently prepared, or without being prepared at all, he will naturally be bitterly disappointed.

Those readers who, whether through laziness or zeal, do not work gradually towards their own personal perfection, and who, though they have made the theoretical knowledge their own, have still achieved nothing in practice, should especially attach great importance to my words. Nothing else but practice makes perfect. Even though the way may be very arduous and progress brought about little by little, patience, perseverance and endurance must nevertheless be applied under all circumstances so that the work may bear fruit.

The Kabbalist who is engaged in numerical combinations will come to regard 462 as a secret number in Kabbalah, one to which any formula must be numerically transferred. For purposes of manifestation in the material world and regardless of the key being used, the number 2 is analogous to the Akasha principle, 60 to the mental and 400 to the astral kingdom. If, therefore, one seeks to bring about the absolute realization of his wishes, he must transfer the respective formula:

twice into the Akasha principle,
60 times into the mental kingdom or body, and
400 times into the astral kingdom or astral body.

Rituals, too, must normally be repeated 462 times, in order to make the necessary volting strong enough so that it will work automatically.

Step XI

The Kabbalistic Use of Divine Names and Beings

Having described the keys and their analogies, I shall now introduce the Kabbalist (in order to deepen his spirit) into one of the most profound secrets of the Kabbalah — the Kabbalistic use of divine names and beings. Before I go into detail, let the Kabbalist be aware of the great Kabbalistic principle, namely that energies — such as, for instance, the elements, the electromagnetic fluid, and to some extent even a certain aspect of the Akasha principle — are to be valued as *quantities* and must not be confounded with *qualities*. However, everything which represents an energy also exists materially, no matter how subtle its form, and must therefore be regarded as matter.

Thus might, virtues, attributes, and abilities all constitute qualities and must not be confused with energy. The Kabbalist must know the difference well if he does not want to make a mistake — which, unfortunately, often occurs with many students of the Kabbalah. Therefore this basic principle should never be confused when working Kabbalistically with letters.

Whenever the subject matter is in regards to a quantity or energy, whether elemental or fluid, it is always a substance. When working with formulas, this principle is of great significance, and there is a great difference as to whether an energy is being used, increased or transferred into the Akasha, in the mental, astral or physical — whether in the form of volts or vibrations, etc. — or whether that same energy is embodied into the mental, astral or material bodies of oneself or of others.

Mights of various kinds, virtues, attributes and abilities, whether used in the Akasha principle, in the mental, astral or material world, may take place without the accumulation of energy or substance; they may unknowingly be raised to the level of quantities. If this is the case, the increased abilities attempt somehow to realize themselves, and hence they automatically expend a particular amount of their analogous energy. This procedure always takes place at the cost of the relevant vitality of the mental, astral or material body, sometimes even at the cost of destiny.

Most religious systems, and often the so-called systems of initiation as well, disregard this principle and occupy themselves primarily with virtues, attributes or abilities without making use of the analogous substance of quantity — the energy substance, the substance of life — of the virtue or ability which is to be increased. This great fundamental mistake naturally causes bad after-effects, including serious disharmonies, failures, setbacks, or even various health disturbances which in turn may lead to pathological states. Thus, if a Kabbalist increases one or several abilities in his mental, astral or physical body, whether by Kabbalah or some other kind of magical operation (such as a ritual or a suggestion meant to influence the subconscious) without supplying the relevant attributes with the necessary energy — i.e., the emanation of energy — the practice must sooner or later lead to failures or other undesirable influences.

In many lodges of initiates, regardless of the system, various kinds of concomitant phenomena or experiences such as visions, hallucinations, ecstatic raptures, and so on are quite often recorded and erroneously interpreted as a certain degree of maturity in one's spiritual development, whereas the practitioner has, in fact, only actually achieved an increase in certain virtues. That this attitude is wrong will at once be clear to the true Kabbalist who knows, masters and considers the universal laws and is able to apply them correctly. Any utilization of Kabbalistic formula magic must be qualitative as well as quantitative in order not to result in one-sided development.

A small example may demonstrate the difference between quality and quantity. A strong, muscular type of man need not always have the qualities corresponding to his strength or muscular power; and, vice versa, a slim man who is quite capable of taking up any of the asana positions of the greatest yogis need not necessarily have their abilities. This example may suffice to illustrate that abilities must not be confused with strength.

Therefore, in the preceding steps the Kabbalist has been taught to apply the letter analogies or formulas qualitatively as well as quantitatively. The preparatory exercises described in my first book, *Initiation into Hermetics*, have taught him the art of condensation as distinct from the art of accumulating energies quantitatively; these energies can only be brought into harmony qualitatively after they have been mastered.

This little digression has been very important because the true Kabbalist works qualitatively as well as quantitatively.

All the divine and other names of angels, archangels, principals, genii, etc., which have been passed down for generations have a quantitative strength and a qualitative might — attributes, abilities, virtues, etc., — provided they have been gained in a truly Kabbalistic way, through tradition or through personal practical experience. These principles must always be held in consideration when working with the Kabbalistic divine names, in order that the true Kabbalist may avoid the mistake made by so many others — namely, to imagine the divine name of an angel, genius, etc., as a personified entity equipped with its ascribed abilities and spheres of operation, etc.

It is, however, customary to imagine that the total complex of a certain formula — a certain number of letters — represents a personified being, which is certainly correct from the magical point of view, since the total complex of powers and abilities is analogous to a certain form and is thus identified with a personified being; for otherwise a being could not be represented. For that which has no shape, no power or ability, does not exist in the whole of creation. However, the Kabbalist also knows that the combined letters representing a being are, at the same time, a Kabbalistic formula having an analogous connection to powers and attributes or describing the relevant personified being respectively.

The practicing Kabbalist must take this into consideration, for a magician who evokes a being calls forth the total complex, the total form representing the relevant powers and abilities — that is, quantities as well as qualities, as such. Therefore the magician evokes the being with its full name — the total complex, qualitatively and quantitatively — which then appears externally in its respective qualities and quantities. In my second book, *The Practice of Magical Evocation*, in which I describe the attributes of the individual beings, I have mentioned that they appear symbolically in accordance with their attributes. That is why the different forms of beings exist, because they are analogous to the different attributes.

A magician and Kabbalist who knows the universal laws and their analogies may at once determine the analogies or symbolic expression of the being on account of its appearance. This is also the reason why, for instance, a being of Venus that has the analogies equivalent to Venus is not able to assume the symbolic appearance of a being of Saturn.

If, therefore, the Kabbalist wants to work with divine names Kabbalistically, i.e., to make the analogous powers and virtues of the same qualitatively and quantitatively his own, he will not use the whole name at once, for this would mean evoking the total key, the whole being; rather, he will make use of the name, as a total complex, letter by letter.

If, for example, he chooses the commonly used angelic name Gabriel, he will not utter it Kabbalistically all at once in its total complex, but will divide it into its letters.

Depending on the key he wants to work with — whether the one-letter, two-letter, three-letter or four-letter key — the Kabbalist will proceed as described when dealing with formulas of the elements. He will transfer part of the name, with either one or two letters, into the Akasha principle and the rest of the letters into the mental, astral and material kingdoms, which means that he is able to transfer, qualitatively or quantitatively, one, two or three letters of the name into each plane depending on the intended Kabbalistic use of the quality or quantity of the name chosen.

With this key in hand, the Kabbalist is thus capable of dividing the name of a being by letters, qualitatively as well as quantitatively, and using it Kabbalistically. Considering this, one will realize that the sphere of power of each being of whatever plane is analogous to its name. The division of the name of a being and its transfer into the desired plane — the mental, astral or material world — and the application of the individual letters of the being's name is called the "true Kabbalistic use of divine names."

The difference between a magician and a Kabbalist is that the magician works with the total complex of powers and mights, quantitatively as well as qualitatively, as a whole being, while the Kabbalist divides the name of a being and uses it by means of the various keys, qualitatively as well as quantitatively, in the Akashic, mental, astral or material plane. Through this the Kabbalist attains the same powers — which quantitatively equal might, abilities, virtues, attributes, etc. — while qualitatively he uses those powers without being in contact with the total complex, i.e. with the formed being.

This fundamental rule differentiates magic from Kabbalah; for the magician calls forth the desired being, or somehow transfers himself into its sphere, or attempts to achieve contact with the being in some passive manner in order to attain the desired powers or effects, whereas the Kabbalist uses the names of beings as key words and, with the help of Kabbalah, appropriates to himself that which can be brought about by the total complex of the being that has been evoked, and thereby he achieves the same effects.

This goes to show that magic, although easier, depends on the total complex of a being. If, on the other hand, the Kabbalist makes use of a being's name as his key word or formula, he will be able, by himself, to bring about anything which that being might achieve.

An initiate must, at any rate, be able to master both magic and Kabbalah, and will usually employ a being only when, due to lack of time, he cannot deal with a matter himself and must therefore entrust the task to a being. If the Kabbalist wants to make the abilities or powers of a being his own, he will use the being's name as a formula.

In this book, I shall refrain from repeating once again the names of the beings of the ten spheres of our universe. The Kabbalist who wants to appropriate to himself the powers and mights of each spiritual being in a qualitative and quantitative manner will find the exact procedure in my second book, *The Practice of Magical Evocation,* in which I deal with the names of the principals, genii, etc., of the individual spheres together with their spheres of operation.

If, therefore, the Kabbalist wants to possess the ability of any principal, he must apply the name of that principal in a Kabbalistic manner, according to the four-letter key, the key to realization, which must be applied in accordance with the Akasha principle, the mental, astral or material plane.

A minor exception, which I did not mention in my second work, is the case of the Shemhamephorash, the seventy-two genii of Mercury who have a very particular analogous connection to the spiritual body. The Shemhamephorash also contains the mystery of the name of God composed of seventy-two letters by which — according to Hebrew Kabbalah — the longest name of God is identified as the highest mode of expression of the deity.

The names of the seventy-two genii of the Mercury Zone express only their qualities and not their quantities or energy-substance, which effect realization in the material plane. The quantities of the seventy-two genii are given expression by the four-letter key and are expressed as a four-letter name of God. The quantitative form or combination of letters always indicates the superior divine name of God of the particular genius.

Many writings dealing with the seventy-two genii or Shem-hamephorash do indicate the superior name of God, but its true meaning or key is not revealed. I shall therefore cite the quantity key or energy key which is expressed by the names of God of the seventy-two genii of the Mercury Zone, one by one.

The first genius, Vehuiah, has the energy-key name of JHVH. The name Vehuiah thus gives expression to the qualitative form. The quantity key or key to the substance of energy is expressed by the four-letter key, the Jod-He-Vau-He.

In the following list I specify, one after the other, all seventy-two genii, with their first names in the first column comprising the quality key, and their names of God in the next column as the quantity key or key of energy substance.

	Quality Key	Quantity Key
1	Vehuiah	Jod-He-Vau-He
2	Jeliel	Aydi
3	Sitael	Schiha
4	Elemiah	Alla
5	Mahasiah	Toth

	Quality Key	Quantity Key
6	Lelahel	Abgd
7	Achaiah	Dodo
8	Kahetel	Moti
9	Aziel	Agzi
10	Aladiah	Sipi
11	Lauviah	Deus
12	Hahaiah	Zeus
13	Jezalel	Boog
14	Mebahel	Dios
15	Hariel	Idio
16	Hakamiah	Dieu
17	Lanoiah	Goth
18	Kaliel	Boog
19	Leuviah	Bogi
20	Pahaliah	Tios
21	Nelekael	Bueg
22	Jeiaiel	Good
23	Melahel	Dieh
24	Hahuiah	Esar
25	Nith-Haiah	Orsi
26	Haaiah	Agdi
27	Jerathel	Teos
28	Séeiah	Adad
29	Reiiel	Zimi
30	Omael	Tusa

	Quality Key	Quantity Key
31	Lekabel	Teli
32	Vasariah	Anot
33	Jehuiah	Agad
34	Lehahiah	Aneb
35	Kevakiah	Anup
36	Menadel	Alla
37	Aniel	Abda
38	Haamiah	Agla
39	Rehael	Goot
40	Ieiazel	Goed
41	Hahahel	Gudi
42	Mikael	Biud
43	Veubiah	Solu
44	Ielahiah	Bosa
45	Sealiah	Hoba
46	Ariel	Piur
47	Asaliah	Kana
48	Mihael	Zaca
49	Vehuel	Mora
50	Daniel	Pola
51	Hahasiah	Bila
52	Imamiah	Abag
53	Nanael	Obra
54	Nithael	Bora
55	Mebaiah	Alai

	Quality Key	Quantity Key
56	Poiel	Illi
57	Nemamiah	Popa
58	Jeialel	Para
59	Harahel	Ella
60	Mizrael	Gena
61	Umabel	Sila
62	Jah-Hel	Suna
63	Amianuel	Miri
64	Mehiel	Alli
65	Damabiah	Tara
66	Manakel	Pora
67	Eiaiel	Bogo
68	Habuiah	Deos
69	Rochel	Deos
70	Jabamiah	Aris
71	Haiel	Zeut
72	Mumiah	Kalo

In a magical evocation, the being — genius, principal, etc. — as a qualitative total complex is called forth in the way described in my book on magical evocation. In the Kabbalistic application, however, the last two letters of the names — i.e., either "el" or "ah" — are omitted. By adding these two letters to the names, the specification of divine qualities is given better expression. From the Kabbalistic point of view, the first genius thus should not be called Vehuiah but merely Vehui; the second genius not Jeliel but only Jeli; the third genius Sita instead of Sitael, and so forth. The Psalms, which, according to many Kabbalistic books, are to be regarded as evocations of a respective genius, should not be valued as Kabbalistic formulas but as mantras of evocation, prayer and meditation.

The other spiritual beings, from the zone girdling the earth up to the sphere of Saturn, bear their quantitative as well as their qualitative attributes in the individual letters of their names. Therefore I did not give any detailed explanations thereof in my second book, *The Practice of Magical Evocation*, and I shall refrain from specifying the other spheres in this book.

The number of letters of a being's name that are to be transferred into the Akasha principle, the mental, astral or material world depends on the wish to be realized. This choice remains entirely with the Kabbalist.

The explanation of the third Tarot card consists of the unveiling of the keys, but not the specification of an individual method. The Kabbalist who has mastered the practices detailed in my second book will be in a position to apply the Kabbalistic keys in a versatile manner. He will be able to divide all names of God, names of angels, etc., Kabbalistically, letter by letter, and to apply the formulas at his discretion in regards to the four Kabbalistic keys. He is thus given a great field of operation and his studies will be inexhaustible in this respect.

In this, the eleventh step, which I conclude herewith, I have shown the Kabbalist how he may apply, in practice, the laws of the cosmic language with regard to the names of God, angels, genii and principals, etc.

Step XII
The Kabbalist as Absolute Master of the Microcosm and the Macrocosm

With the preceding step, the practical development and training of the perfect Kabbalist has been, so to speak, completed. In this step, the twelfth and last of this work, I want to review how the whole system is organized and give a summary of the whole course.

Above all, the Kabbalist should have convinced himself that preparation through the concentration exercises of the three senses outlined in my first work, *Initiation into Hermetics,* has been very necessary in order to achieve a certain degree of concentration of all three senses for a certain period of time, which then enables one to utter a letter Kabbalistically, to work creatively therewith.

The Kabbalist has been taught, step by step, how to impregnate his mental, astral and physical bodies by means of single letters, in order not only to take in certain vibrations within himself but to evoke these in the different planes. Furthermore, he has been taught by frequent repetitions and practical exercises to give a letter the dynamics or power of expansion necessary for his Kabbalistic work; likewise, he has attained the ability to work inductively and deductively, to condense and de-condense in such a way as to be effective in the mental matrix or mental kingdom, the astral matrix or astral kingdom, and in the physical body or material world. With this work, he has acquired for himself not only the quantitative ability of expansion of the mental, astral and material bodies, but also the ability to give the individual powers or quantities their analogous qualities. Not until he has learned this will the letter uttered by the Kabbalist become magical, dynamic and thus creatively effective.

Thereby he has enlivened the regions appertaining to the elements, strengthened the powers therein in correspondence to the universal powers and their analogies, and thus brought them into harmony with each other. His microcosm — the miniature world — has been brought into perfect harmony with the macrocosm, and the Kabbalist has taken full account of this lawfulness in accordance with the *Emerald Tablet of Hermes,* which says: "That which is above is like that which is below."

Having attained the ability of being effective mentally, astrally and materially, he has become absolute Master of the Word in all three kingdoms. Nothing is impossible for a Kabbalist who, like the Creator, can create everything with the Word. This means that with the Word he is able to bring about any effect on a small scale, i.e., in the microcosm; and if necessary, and if Divine Providence permits or so orders, on the larger scale or macrocosm as well.

Furthermore, the Kabbalist has learned to build up volts Kabbalistically, to know all the lawfulness and the analogous correspondences with regard to the microcosm and the macrocosm, and also to master them. His abilities and powers have increased tremendously and cannot be described by mere words. It stands to reason that his responsibility has increased thereby too. For as soon as a formula is transferred into the Akasha principle, cause and effect are no longer subject to destiny but exclusively to the Highest Divine Providence. A true Kabbalist and true magician (for magic and Kabbalah go together) who has achieved this state of maturity will never lend himself to merely fulfilling the material wishes of others or gaining personal advantage from the knowledge which he practices. His sublime wish will be to serve humankind and, veiled in silence and deepest humility, he will never show off his maturity.

He will not be induced by any situation to violate the laws of divine order. Although he is able to do anything, he will always do what Divine Providence orders him to do, for he is a servant of God and a high initiate.

Usually, a Kabbalist who has proceeded thus far is entrusted with a high mission to humankind, or he is given the opportunity to further increase his consciousness by penetrating deeply into the so-called spheric Kabbalah, which has to do with the application of cosmic formulas with regard to the remaining planes. Thus the Kabbalist will be able to go beyond the four-letter key and will be initiated into the further pages of the Book of Wisdom — the Tarot cards — not only theoretically but also in a practical sense, providing he conscientiously follows the will of Divine Providence.

A spheric Kabbalist who is able to work Kabbalistically as well as cosmically can neither be understood nor comprehended by ordinary mortals and immature people. Having reached this stage, the Kabbalist neither needs personal guidance nor a book of instructions, specifications and keys. Such an initiate is already a true adept and neither a book nor a mortal being can tell him anything. Since he has achieved the highest perfection, it is then up to him alone to dissolve his "I" consciousness in Divine Providence in all Its aspects.

However, before such a state of perfection is achieved, the further pages of the Book of Wisdom have to be worked through practically. I have not been permitted to reveal these and make them accessible through systematic working methods, for humankind is not yet sufficiently mature to grasp such profound mysteries of Divine Providence, their basis, and to accept and assimilate them intellectually. Certain laws cannot be at all comprehended by mere intellect and can only be understood from the standpoint of wisdom with the personal universal consciousness.

I should, however, be very pleased if I were permitted by Divine Providence to reveal at least two more pages of the Book of Wisdom in order to help the most gifted ones on their path. But it is left to Divine Providence alone to decide.

Epilogue

My gratitude is due to Divine Providence for having endowed me with the energy necessary to complete my task, which was to describe the first three Tarot cards or pages of the Book of Wisdom, and to compile the universal methods, derived from my own practice, for practical application by my readers.

As I am not an author by profession, and as I have done this in addition to colossal efforts undertaken for the sake of suffering humankind, it has not been easy for me to write down, in simple words, the highest of all sciences representing the lawfulness of the highest universal truths, and to convey it to readers, especially to all seekers of truth.

The many letters of gratitude that I have received from enthusiastic readers are the best proof of the fact that, until now, no volume has appeared in the book trade which describes the path to true perfection in such an open and intelligible manner.

My mission, however, was not to satisfy the personal wishes of individuals, but to show the ways and means to those who are interested in their personal perfection, so that they may, at times, use their acquired abilities for the betterment of their existence.

Everyone must walk the path by himself; no one else can do his work for him. My books, written in a clear and intelligible language, will be the safest guide for everyone. But whoever aims only to attain a better level of existence will never achieve what he desires; for these books have not been written for the purpose of merely procuring wealth, prosperity, and fulfillment of all one's personal wishes, but for the purpose of making the reader steadfast and successful in his struggles in life.

On earth, every human being has two teachers: firstly, him or herself, and secondly, destiny. What man is unable to achieve through his own diligence, practice, renunciation, pain, grief, etc., will be presented to him by destiny through disappointments and vicissitudes. Life is a school, not an amusement park. Over and over again, man on this earth is challenged to learn, to develop, and to perfect himself. He may enjoy the good; he should learn from the evil; but he must never give up, for nothing on this globe happens without good reason: everything that befalls him happens for a purpose, and always at the right time. In the end, it is up to man himself to encounter all events courageously and to gain a wealth of knowledge therefrom for his own development.

I hereby express my cordial thanks to all my readers for their acknowledgments. Should I have succeeded in showing interested readers the path to perfection by having enriched their knowledge, my mission has been wholly accomplished, even if only a few should muster the great perseverance necessary to attain the requisite state of maturity.

The Author

The Works of
Franz Bardon

Note to the Reader

This series of books on Hermetics (Alchemy) reveals the Holy Mysteries. They are unique in that they contain the theory as well as the practice. It is also important that these works be read and practiced in the proper order. Should the reader not do so, he will have great difficulties in understanding the contents, even from a philosophical point of view; as for the practitioner, he will not progress at all. Therefore it is advisable for everyone to follow this sequence:

1. Frabato the Magician
2. Initiation into Hermetics (Volume I)
3. The Practice of Magical Evocation (Volume II)
4. The Key to the True Kabbalah (Volume III)
5. Franz Bardon: Questions & Answers and the Great Arcanum
6. Memories of Franz Bardon

Frabato the Magician

Though cast in the form of a novel, Frabato is in fact the spiritual autobiography of Franz Bardon, one of the greatest adepts in the universe.

Set in Dresden, Germany, in the early 1930s, the story chronicles Bardon's magical battles with the members of a powerful black lodge, his escape from Germany during the final days of the Weimar Republic, and the beginning of the spiritual mission which was to culminate in Bardon's classic books on Hermetic magic. Also included are fragments of The Golden Book of Wisdom, the fourth Tarot Card. Photos.

Initiation into Hermetics
(Vol. I of The Holy Mysteries)

A course of magical instruction in ten steps. Theory and practice. Complete revelation of the first Tarot card. From the index:

Part I: Theory

The picture of the magician. About the elements Fire, Air, Water and Earth. Light. The Akasha or etheric principle. Karma, the law of cause and effect. The soul or astral body. The astral plane. The spirit. The mental plane. Truth. Religion. God.

Part II: Practice

1) Thought control. Subordination of unwanted thoughts. Self-knowledge or introspection. Conscious breathing and reception of food.
2) Auto-suggestion. Concentration exercises with the five senses. Meditations. Attaining astral and magical balance with respect to the elements. Transmutation of character and temperament.
3) Concentration exercises with two or three senses at once. Inhaling the elements through the whole body. Impregnation of space.

4) Transference of consciousness. Accumulation of elements. Production of elemental harmony. Rituals and their practical application.
5) Space magic. Outward projection of the elements. Preparation for passive communication with the invisible ones.
6) Preparation to master the Akasha principle. Conscious induction of trance by means of the Akasha. Conscious creation of different beings (elementals, larvae, phantoms).
7) Development of the astral senses by means of the elements: clairvoyance, clairaudience, clairsentience. Creation of elementaries. Magical animation of pictures.
8) The practice of mental wandering. Mastering the electric and magnetic fluids. Magical influence by means of the elements. Preparation of a magic mirror.
9) The practical use of the magic mirror: clairvoyance, distant effects, different tasks of projection, etc. Deliberate separation of the astral body from the physical one. Magical charging of talismans, amulets and gems.
10) Elevation of the spirit to higher spheres or worlds. Conscious communication with God. Communication with spirit beings. One picture of the first Tarot card. One photo of the author.

The Practice of Magical Evocation
(Vol. 2 of The Holy Mysteries)

Complete revelation of the second Tarot card. Instructions for evoking spirit beings from the spheres surrounding us. The author speaks from his own experience!

Part I: Magic
Magical aids: the magic circle, triangle, censer, mirror, lamp, wand, sword, crown, garment, and belt. The pentacle, lamen or seal. The book of magic spells. In the domain of the spirit beings. Advantages and disadvantages of evocational magic. The *spiritus familiaris* or serving spirit. The magical evocation. The practice of magical evocation (description of a complete conjuration).

Part II: Hierarchy
1) The Spirits of the Four Elements.
2) Intelligences of the zone girdling the earth.
3) The 360 heads of the zone girdling the earth.
4) Intelligences of the Moon sphere.
5) The 72 intelligences of the Mercury sphere.
6) Intelligences of the Venus sphere.
7) Genii of the Sun sphere.
8) Intelligences of the Mars sphere.
9) Genii of the Jupiter sphere.
10) The Saturn sphere.
11) The spheres of Uranus and Pluto.
12) Communication with spirit beings, genii and intelligences of all spheres through mental traveling.
13) Talismanic magic.

Part III: Illustrations — Seals of Spirit Beings
One picture of the second Tarot card, including 148 pages with seals of spirit beings.

Franz Bardon: Questions & Answers
And The Great Arcanum
By Dieter Rüggeberg

First published in 2008, this volume is the first complete new work to appear since Bardon's famous series of books on Hermetics. Compiled by Dieter Rüggeberg from the notes of Bardon's students in Prague, it represents his oral teachings on the nature of the magical universe. Set in the form of questions and answers, this book is an invaluable addition to the Bardon material. The newly discovered charts of the elements have been incorporated into this new edition to give the reader a complete and concise insight into the negative and positive characteristics as defined by the four elements.